PROBLEM OF PEACE-MAKING IN MIZORAM

About the Editor

Prof. J.V. Hluna finished his M.A. (History) in 1974 and got his Ph.D. in 1986 from Gauhati. He is one of the founder-lecturers of Government Aizawl College in 1975. Hluna joined Pachhunga University College in 1977. He founded Government Hrangbana College in 1980 and became first Secretary in the Governing Board. He is also the Founder-Principal of Government T. Romana College in 1994. He was the first to be offered Professorship in undergraduate college by Mizoram University (Central) in 2011. He has presented many research papers and articles, and has also written and edited several books in English and Mizo.

PROBLEM OF PEACE-MAKING IN MIZORAM

Lal Hmingthanga

Edited By
J.V. Hluna

CONCEPT PUBLISHING COMPANY PVT. LTD.
NEW DELHI-110059

ISBN-13 : 978-81-8069-962-7

First Published 2013

Published and Printed by

Concept
Since 1974

Concept Publishing Company Pvt. Ltd.
A/15-16, Commercial Block, Mohan Garden
New Delhi-110059 (India)
T : 25351460, 25351794, *F* : 091-11-25357109
E: publishing@conceptpub.com, *W*: www.conceptpub.com
Editorial Office: H-13, Bali Nagar, New Delhi-110 015, India.

Cataloging in Publication Data--Courtesy: D.K. Agencies (P) Ltd. <docinfo@dkagencies.com>

Hmingthanga, Lal, 1934-1995.
Problem of peace-making in Mizoram / Lal Hmingthanga ; edited by J.V. Hluna.
p. cm.
Includes bibliographical references and index.
ISBN 9788180699627

1. Ethnic conflict—India—Mizoram. 2. Lushai (Asian people)—India—Mizoram Politics and government. 3. Mizoram (India)—Politics and government. 4. Reconciliation. 5. Peace-building—India—Mizoram. I. Hluna, John V. (John Vânlal), 1947- II. Title.

DDC 305.800954166 23

Preface

In writing this small book, my object is to give explanations to the people of India and friends in other parts of the world in their misgivings of the unhappy situation in Mizoram and the stand of Mizo people. I am afraid, my pre-occupancy with reports of the Indian military atrocity that come everyday might have driven me too much in that line. I request my readers to amend themselves such excessive, if any.

At the time, India is having much internal strife and unpleasantness, violent demonstrations are common features of the daily papers. Public wills are blackmailed in the Assembly Halls: crossing Assembly floor is a common scene. The twenty years old Congress monopoly Government at the Central hangs in uncertain balance, since the coming up of the Non-Congress Government in a number of States. President's Rule, the last measure of the Central Government, are imposed in a number of States. Only a few State Governments could be saved from the confusion. The Anti-Hindi of South and the Hindi-portagonists of the North are furiously demonstrating for their respective objectives. Both of them seem to be growing apart. The wild-fire discontent of the people in various parts of India are a good food for Communism. The hills and plains people of Assam are antigonising one another, and the political gap is sure to separate them. Kashmir dispute, the Twenty years old itch of India and Pakistan, finds new feet in the release of Mohamad Sheikh Abdullah, the Lion of Kashmir comes out of its barred case. Pakistan repeatedly accused her of exterminating Muslim minority in India. Chinese involvement in Kerala, Bengal, and Assam is suspected. The three-year old peaceful negotiation between India and Federal Government of Nagaland is nearing impasse. The Maharaja of Sikkim wanted a revision of his country's relation with India. He wants more development of his country and for his people. He has an American wife. The Punjab's Master Tara Singh was dead, but Pubjab is not dead. Tamil land of the South seems looking for a chance. And then, Kashmir?

India, under the present circumstances is like a worm-eaten house which may collapse any time one post or another post under the black magic charm of the Indian Democracy. Mrs. Indira Gandhi is harping dolefully for national integration but millions of her unresponsive people find it hard to dance in harmony under her magic flute which has lost its charms due to the complexity of the Indian Democracy. Right or wrong, it is the felt duty of the Indian leaders to save the integrity of India, at any cost.

So far as India is concerned, Mizo people look the chaotic condition with uneasy minds for it can have repercussion in her dealings with the people of Mizoram.

They, therefore, wish India more stability in the Government and a strong leadership to reason a better solution of Mizoram with dignity and honour. They further wish the people of India's to impress their leaders to deal every state of affairs with firmness in the right. Mizo people are keenly desiring Indian leaders to have proper frame of mind and not to indulge in depravation of Mizo people and vivisection of their country for her political gain.

India is a great country. It is the world's biggest Democratic show-case. It is one of the voices of the world anxious to hear in any event of crises in any part of the world. However, the Indian complexity in her diplomatic dealing with certain neighbouring countries forms a complex feature:

KASHMIR: In regard to the Kashmir affairs, at least more than three international agreements were signed with the U.N.O. and Pakistan respectively for a free plebiscite without interference of arms. Uptill now, the Kashmiri people cannot have chance to determine for themselves, even after two wars were fought in Kashmir with Pakistan. Within this period, India seems to have done much in her favour. Meanwhile, the Indian leaders, time and again stated that India wants talk with Pakistan to settle the outstanding problem between the two including Kashmir dispute, while, on the other hand, it stated that Kashmir is the integral part of India and thus no one country should interfere in the internal affairs of India. Pakistan also stated that she wants talks with India at any time, but such talks should be meaningful. The famous Tashkent Declaration signed between India and Pakistan under a Russian host after the September War in Kashmir in 1965, has had no fruitful result. One side accused the other for violation of the Tashkent Agreement and ended with it. Too much of playing in the delaying tactics may lead to another war. I hope and pray that another war of Kashmir should not come. Meanwhile, it is high time to amend one's intention.

BURMA : The Indo-Burma relation had never been good as it is now-a-days. In the years preceding to 1965, many Indian nationals living in Burma were driven out. In 1965, when the national aspiration of the Mizo people was eminent, the Indian Prime Minister late Mr. Lal Bahadur Shastri had gone over to Rangoon. One cannot say the motive of the Indian leader; but one thing came out of the visit was an agreement between the two countries—non-interference in the internal affairs of others. It is difficult to say that this has implication with the affairs of Mizo people; but one cannot sit off-handedly. Burma, under General Newin's Revolutionary Council, pursues its socialist programme of land reform, industrialization and social welfare beginning in 1963, the people of Chin Hills State feel displeasure about such change. The contented Chin Hills leaders organized reactionary movement against the Revolutionary Council. Some of them, came down over to Mizoram and I happened to meet one of them, who was the leader. I feel lucky because we speak the same language. I asked his political objective but he gave no definite answer. Chin Hills Independence? No, during the discourse I could guess that they want to put back the hands of the Burma Revolutionary programme to its pre-socialist programme. The Chin Hills people, in fact, had no political outlook by the time and their leader were embarrassed. One thing very clear was that they were very much discontented with the change under the Revolutionary Council. They had contacts with some Government of India's high officials and in a few months later, few Chin Hills youngmen were armed and were able to attack police posts in Chin Hills. From where they got their arms was the question; but one thing was sure that when they were coming down they did not bring arms with them. In the meantime, a huge arms and ammunition were rushed by the Indian troops to Champhai, the last Indian post near Burma border. A few months after this, India and Burma could sign agreement on non-interference in the other's internal affairs. Now that India and Burma had the agreement; consequence on it, the Revolutionary Council of Burma arrested more than a thousand refugees who fled to Burma due to Indian military repressive measures in 1966. So far as Burma is concerned, we have the Chin Hills regulation the law is being enforced since the British rule in Mizoram. This law provides for the Mizo people facility of visiting each other across the border within 24 miles radius from the boundary. Inter-marriage across the border is still going on.

NAGAS : The Naga people demand independence from India since 1947. After a prolonged fighting between the Indian troop and Nagaland Federal Government forces a cease-fire was reached in 1963, as a result of peace mission works organized by Nagaland Baptist Church. Rev. Michael Scot of England, Mr. B.P. Chaliha of Assam and Mr. Jay Prakash Narayan, Sarvodaya leader, were the peace mission members. After a series of talks between the two leaders there cannot be substantial improvement on the question of Naga demand for Sovereignty and the solution of the problem still lies in a mist. The Naga Nationalist demand Government of India to make way for international observers from neutral countries to examine the case of the Nagas *vis-à-vis* the Indian stand, but India objected the idea. Not only that, the Government of India expelled Rev. Michael Scot from Nagaland and India. Naga people want peace with honour and on the basis of mutual respects; but India desires to solve the Naga problem with justice—justice within her own terms.

CHINA : The Sino-India friendship and *Panchsheel* (five principles of co-existence) were short lived. In the 1962 conflict between China and India on the roof of the world was a test of Chinese strength. The conflict is a boon to Indian defence. Ever since then, her defence is greatly strengthened with the help of American arms. India is the biggest non-aligned country and she thus know how to use being non-aliance. She has long and lasting friendship with Russia, and thus gets MIG fighters in spite of her being a biggest democratic country in the world. The U.S.S.R. has deep interest in India and that is all. As a champion of Democracy, she looks after the Tibetan refugees who fled over to India as a result of rebellion against China. Dalai Lama, the God-King of Tibet is well looked after in India; recognition of him as head of Tibet is still a likely question in the Indian Parliament, Government of People's Republic of China accused India of helping the Tibetan rebellion against the People's Government in Tibet. In 1967 conflict in the Sikkim border, China accused India again of her political scheming. The people's daily news, the New China News Agency, said that that was planned with the Deputy Prime Minister, Mr. Morarji Desai's trip to Washington for more arms aid. Not so long before, the ruler of Sikkim stated his country's, willingness for a revision of his country's relation with India. As a result of the conflict, India rushed in troops and then, Sikkim was under military emergency.

We had a number of meetings with the Indian leaders and Government high officials during 1964-1966 (till March), their attitude was evasive to the basic question concerning the rights of the Mizo people per their memorandum of 1965. In fact, they had never given heed to the demand of the Mizo people. They have had their own designs; the design of Special Development Scheme of Mizoram, with it the Indian armies were moving into Mizoram. A number of letters and telegrams were sent to Indian Prime Minister and the Assam State Chief Minister explaining the urgency of the Indian situation and talks between the Indian leaders and Mizo leaders were demanded for discussion over the matter. India paid no heed. Mr. Laldenga, President of the Mizo National Front, had a last talk with the Chief Minister of Assam on 27th February, 1966 through telephone. He requested the Government of India to reconsider its re-enforcement troops on way to Mizoram and pull them back. The Chief Minister said, 'No'.

CHRISTIANITY : Life of Christianity in Mizoram is about 70 years. Missionaries from Great Britain brought the Gospel to this hill and isolated land in the South East Asia in about 1900. All the people in Mizoram, except a few nomadic tribes along the Chittagong Hill Tracts, are Christians. The Missionaries, along their Gospel work, took up every economic development of the people. Education and other charity institutions, were run by them. Christianity in Mizoram, is, now, a bedrock of their culture. Christianity, thus, has preponderance in their social and economic outlook. The Gospel gives them understanding of humane principles, so does in politics.

It is only two decades since the people have political ideas and party system. In such a short time, it is difficult to thoroughly associate with the democratic ideas. But the Mizo people with their Christian outlook could well associate with the democratic frame of ideas and in early sixties their political consciousness reached a high level. This consciousness is greatly enhanced by their understanding of human principles in the light of Christian outlook.

There were contradictions, in the early stage, in their political philosophy as to its consistency with the principles of Christianity. Hindu influence cannot totally be ignored in this. Some politicians are exponents to the view that there are consistency to the political philosophy and Christian beliefs. Some did not subscribe to the idea, having this confusion in mind, I wrote my first book, *Exodus Politiks* (in Mizo) where I elaborately discussed my view on the subject. The book is well accepted by the people and it helps them to a certain length of understanding. To me, the spirit that longs for salvations and life beyond this worldly living is the same spirit that hungers for political freedom on this earth. I was very surprised to know that the Government of India banned my book in 1966. A Government order was issued that anybody is found keeping it or any house, where it is found, is subject to punishment or burnt. My book thus, has to go underground. I received numerous comments from my friends and people wherever I go about the book. The book is intended for giving understanding to the basic principles of politics and its impact on our day-to-day life and how it is ordered with consistency to religious truth.

In regard to tension and complex political situation in Mizoram and great sufferings caused by violent conflict between the Mizo people and the Indian Troops. It is likely that many of our Christian brothers might have misgivings in the state of affairs. Some, perhaps, condemned the revolt in Mizoram as is not compatible with the Principles of Christianity; or on ground of their conceived idea. Yes, most Christians should condemn the use of force, except when it is in self-defence, and it is for the vested interest. Christianity itself is non-violence. Christ plainly says, "My Kingdom is not of this world"; thus, man does not need to fight with weapons for the cause of Christianity in this world. It is not only in Christianity, but men of conscience all over the world should condemn use of force unless it is in self-defence. In Mizoram use of force should be condemned, not only on the side of Mizo people *ex parte*; but on both the parties.

It is a fact, although, that religion and politics can go a long way together, there is limit. Politics should not take help of religion for achieving political end. But in politics, religious interest cannot totally be overlooked. It is harmful if politics takes religious co-ordination and it is equally harmful if religion cannot guide politics. Therefore, it may be necessary to first understand the basic principles of Christianity and politics. So far as man is concerned, they are of a kind for two things. One is for a thing beyond this world, and the other is for this world; but they grow out of the same thing—man. They grow out of the same spirit; they grow out of the same person.

In other words, Religion is a principle of humanity in relation to God. *Bible* (so also the other religious books) is a history—a continuous history revealing the relationship of God and man. *Bible* is, therefore, the way and the truth that man should follow in his pilgrimage to his home in Heaven. The truth transforms into the humane principles, and this prevails in a man's political, social and economical outlook. "Thou shalt love thy neighbour as thyself," is a Christian living. A Christian wants good Government, peace and welfare for others as well as for himself. Colonies are given freedom, so that they may have peace and pursue the way to welfare and happiness. It is Christian that domination should be eliminated from the face of this planet. Freedom in this world is a foretaste of perfect freedom which a Christian is to inherit in his heavenly Kingdom. Therefore, there is nothing wrong for Christian to have political freedom, provided such interests do not clash with the truth. Christianity is non-violence, it endures all things, it then prevails on all things.

Christians are the children of God; it is their obligation to make peace. They sympathise all sufferings of mankind and give help wherever is possible; that is his love for his neighbours as himself. A Christian is a peace-maker. With "loins girt about with truth, and having on the breastplate of righteousness," (Ephesians, 6:14) he needs not afraid of authority. He needs not afraid of power; he must bear his Christian responsibility. He must say what is right and what is wrong. He must not be a bias. He must hate domination, he must hate treachery; he must also hate intrigue; he must be simple with truth. He must not back up wrong authority, and must not do anything for its interest. He must uphold freedom and work for maintenance of peace with honour.

On the other hand, politics is also a principle of humanity in relation to Government. What Government? Democratic Government sets on the will of the people of the world. If a man works on democratic principles he has to follow according to the dictates of humane principles that goes a long way with the religious truth. In politics one should take principles from one's religious conviction. Man's political activity in search of good government where he hopes to attain welfare and happiness is guided by his morality based on his religious belief. A man without religion is a man without hope; such a man is dead.

"Peace on earth, goodwill towards man" is a great significance in the political life of men. Men are in great need of peace, but their search for peace is a complexity. Allied Nations, in Second World War fought with Germany for peace; Hitler exterminated more than six million Jews for peace and prosperity; Arabs want to exterminate the existence of Jews of Israel State; US bombed Hanoi for peace; and, China pursues her programme of International

Communism for world peace with a slogan, "Power grows out of gun barrel". India wants to hold on Mizoram and Nagaland—perhaps for defence strategy. Man's desire and intention is subject to complexity without religious morality. He often astrays. Humanity is, then, suppressed in the name of peace. Minority nationals are exterminated in the name of Democracy. Political fallacy is a cruel persecutor of humanity. Let us, therefore, try hard to uphold the Heavenly message, "Peace on earth, goodwill towards men", in our democracy in accordance with the principles of humanity.

I had a discourse with one missionary worker. He frankly told me that he was not of opinion that the Mizo people should resort to violence in their attempt to achieve their political objective, as it is not in consistency with Christianity. He is right. Nor do I subscribe policy of violence for achieving political objective of any kind. But the logic cannot always prevail. I cannot, in the meantime, say whether a Christian should refrain from using force if such situation compels him. I do not advocate force; I would only discuss how our human problem is solved. If the British refrain from using force against German, what will next come upon the British Nation? If the US refrains from using force against the Communists, what will come next? It is, therefore, the dictates of tension and situation in which a Christian is put to fight gallantly. Now in Mizoram, a true Mizo young man can only be happiest to see a gun in his hand. He does not feel for terylene dressing suits, nor terrylene shirts. He cannot be happy with his girl friend; he has no desire for cinema fun; he has no desire for social entertainment. He left his home and says, "for God and my country", To die for his country cause is the greatest thing he can do in this world; it is his love for his neighbours; it is for peace. He dies a patriot and his death is his country's honour. He cannot be happy to see the cruel repression of his people by Indians. His fight is for peace with honour in Mizoram *vis-à-vis* India.

The Missionary went on saying that he has a country in Heaven and he would not have even fought Germany. Let the German occupy London, Paris or others, they shall never destroy the heavenly country. Yes, Christians are not belonging to this world, they have the next world after this. Life in this world is their necessary pilgrimage. We, therefore, put up our lives and hopes to the next world. Let us call the kingdoms—the religious kingdom and the political kingdom respectively. The two kingdoms have an effective meaning in the Christian life. A Christian desires for welfare. Political kingdom is compatible with the principles of his religious kingdom.

The religious kingdom is a thing difficult to be desired for even for a Christian for we have little knowledge about it. To desire it is to have divine revolution. I still remember to have asked my late old father, when I was a small boy, about this kingdom, which had little attraction to me. The golden city and its furniture had not attracted me much, and I had not, by the time, seen gold or jewel; thus I had no idea how beautiful the city would be like. And I said, "Daddy, what pleasures shall we have in Heaven"? "Well", he said, "It is LOVE". "With love", he went on, "everything is pleasure". "Love will be increased in Heaven much more than on this earth", I think my father is right. About Gold and jewel! Even at this time, I have little desire of them for my furnitures.

We need love not only in our religious kingdom, but also in our political kingdom. A country which has no emotional integrity and common national sentiment is often subject to internal strife and confusion. There are human problems on ground of races, religion, culture, etc. These problems work on political fields. Paucity of Hindu love for Muslim and *vice versa*, is the cause of the creation of India and Pakistan with great cost of human lives. In the same manner, paucity of Hindu love for civilized Mizo-Christian tribal—is the cause of tension and complex political situation in Mizoram. There is no human law good enough to provide solution. Human intentions and wish, however good it may be, is interpreted in a different way, and cannot work on bigamous principles. Truth is greatly hurt. Therefore, would it not be wiser to follow the natural law—that God created men and forms them into many nations.

A Hindu and a Christian are quite different in outlook and thought-forms. The Indian Secularism is a hard born for a Christian to swallow unless he practices bigamy of doctrines. Hindus have multi-gods' one God and this is the central theme of Indian Education which has its purpose in the scheme of Indian National Integration, Christians have one God, that is enough. Indian Education based on the philosophy, "All religions are good" is not an acceptable proposition for Christian. Christians cannot mix up good teachings from *Bible, Koran, Vedas*, etc., nor make any compromise on principles of faith. His *Bible* is the only truth that can lead him to his Heavenly Kingdom. By this we do not dispute with the human values in other religions. Christianity is a principle of humanity in relation to one God. If religions, Christianity and others together, are used to serve the interest of the State and subordinate political objective, it is communistic. Christianity cannot be wedded to other religions. In the meantime, I accept that other religions are not evil in themselves, they contained many values and truth, but they were, nevertheless, imperfect and belonged to uncivilized stage. Even if all other religions make converted effort to boost up State's policy, Christianity shall not participate. Christian belongs to one God and their political interest is in subordination of the interests of their religious kingdom. State interests should be on the back line. We must not mix up religious interest and the political interest. Let live alone the freedom of conscience; for his kingdom is not of this world.

BRITISH RULE : Having occupied India for more than two centuries the British came to Mizoram first in 1871. There were no national boundaries, by the time, in existence in this hill and mountainous regions of South East Asia between Burma on the East and India on the West. There were historical struggle for survival in the form of tribal war; one tribe attempted to dominate the others for extension of its kingdom and the like in a rudimentary form. There was no proper name for national level; each tribe was named after the tribe itself. The British intervened in this process of historical evolution and thus changed the course of their history. Mr. G.A. Grierson C.I.E., D. Litt;

I.C.S.; compiler and publisher of the linguistic Survey of India wrote this people as Kuki-Chin Group and their area of habitat comprises from Naga Hills in the North and Sandway district of Burma in the South; from Myittha River in the east to Bay of Bengal in the West. He did not mention this people as a national group. But he called them linguistic group. His rough estimate of their population was 10,00,000 in 1904. They were not a nation but they were numerous families of different tribes with common tradition, culture and common language. The British had made divisions among the people to suit their administrative convenience. Some parts are cut out and made it a separate administrative area; some parts are annexed to nearest alien administrative headquarters; and the Lushai Hills and Lushais were the outcome of such injustice. Now, therefore, Mizoram comprising about 6,00,000 population in India and the Mizo people for the Lushai Hills and the Lushais respectively are a late political evolution with which the people so dearly call themselves. They are derived from common words 'Zo' and 'Mi' meaning people of the highlands. All of the people in the tribes have their common identity and common language in Mizo and a common heritage in Mizoram. However, the terminology is not necessarily a compulsion to those who do not will themselves. Rather, from the very inception, the political terminology is democratic and should remain so.

The Mizo people were, therefore, independent before the British intervention. Each village formed an independent unit like the Greek-city states. But they had a compact social living. There had been, however, border clashes between Mizo and the neighbouring peoples which ultimately brought the British to the scene in 1871. Three columns of British expedition were sent against Mizoram from Cachar of India, Chittagong side of Pakistan and from Burma on the East. The Mizo people, under independent leadership of their chiefs, put up a stout resistance to the invaders which took more than one decade. Finally, agreements were concluded between the British and the Lushai chiefs which subsequently brought Mizoram under the British colonial rule and annexed to the British Indian Empire in 1889.

During British rule internal administration of the country was solely left to the people. The chief retained their hereditary chieftainship with almost all the privileges enjoyed during the Pre-British period. A political officer known as Superintendent of the Lushai Hills was, however, acting as a unifying chief, who, in turn, acted under a direct responsibility of the Provincial Governor in his capacity as the Crown Representative.

When India attained Dominion status under the promulgation of the Constitution of India Act of 1935, the British Government, having realized the distinct block of Mizo nationality, excluded the Lushai Hills from the purview of the Constitution. The Lushai Hills was then kept as a special Area—EXCLUDED AREA—under the Government Order of 1936. The Internal administration as well as the external relations were under direct responsibility of the Governor-in-Council as the Crown Representative. Thus, Mizoram (then Lushai Hills) had no connection with the British India or the Indian States. The

Government of India and its Parliament has no influence whatsoever in the Lushai Hills. The Indian politics and policies were never known to the Mizo. The position of the Lushai Hills was, in fact, semi-independent; having full autonomy in regard to her internal affairs and that of the external relation controlled by the Governor-General-in-Council as the Crown Representative. During Second World War, as the condition was such, the Lushai chiefs jointly issued a manifesto to give a stout resistance against the Janpanese invasion. Commenting on the manifesto, Mr. M.C. McCall, then Superintendent of the Lushai Hills, stated that the joint declaration made by the Lushai chiefs was nothing less than that of the declaration made by England, Scotland and Wales. He further narrated that the principle of the Atlantic Charter so far as it has concerned about the affairs of the Lushai Hills. The Allied Powers will be held responsible to the affairs of the Mizo people after the war in case of any attempt made by the neighbouring countries to annex the Lushai Hills to their territories against the will of the people.

In the context of the present complex political situation in Mizoram with reference to our choice of temporary integration with the Union of India in 1947 due to the political unconsciousness of the then Mizo leaders and the Indian insufficiency in meeting the genuine offer of the Mizo people to India reserving the rights of self-determination after ten years, the validity of the rights of the Mizo people remains as ever fresh though some people may have abandoned hope for the chance to exercise our rights. India's stand for Mizoram as her internal affairs has no validity and cannot be regarded as removing the just and rightful stand of the Mizo people which has been in existence since the British rule. The case of the Kashmir accession to India cannot be a criterion in the affairs of the Mizo people. They did not sign any accession bill with India.

The British rule in Mizoram lasted for about sixty years. There was much change in social outlook of the people. This was greatly because of the new faith—Christianity to which all are converted. The Missionary has laid the bedrock for the present trend of civilization in Mizoram. The Christian missionary pioneers such as Pu Buanga (J.H. Lorrain) and Sap Upa (F.W. Savidge) are still fresh in the memories of the Mizo people. The early missionaries were of mainly two denominations, the London Baptist Church and the Welsh Presbyterian Church. Up to this present day the churches in Mizoram and those of the foreign churches still maintain relations. I thank the Mizo people would ever respect those Christian churches in Britain of their ideas in respect of both religious and public affairs.

POLITICAL RETROSPECT OF 1946-1950: Consequence on the British Government's pronouncement of the Lushai Hills as a political danger area, the British banned any political activities up to April 1946. Subsequently there was no political institution till the British transferred her power to the Government of free India. The Indian politics has no influence on Mizoram and that when the Indian National Congress fought freedom for Indian Independence the Mizo people has no part in anyway to the cause of India.

At the dawn of Indian Independence the Mizo people were left confused following the inevitability of British departure from Mizoram and Indian political scene. In 1946, political parties were instituted. The major party was Mizo Union. This was the first political party ever set up in Mizoram. The manifestos of the party were such as the abolition of the Lushai Chieftainship, abolition of impressed coolie, abolition of tithes paid to the chiefs and other such privileges enjoyed by the Lushai chiefs. The main policy of the party had been integration with the Indian Union. But the majority of the Mizo people are not of the same policy though, however, enthused by the party's propaganda about overthrowing the chiefs. In these affairs many suspected the Indian National Congress' hands playing from behind which was then followed by resignation of some of top members of party officials and a partition within the high command of the party. Mr. Macdonald, then Superintendent of the Lushai Hills issued a statement calling upon the Mizo people to fully aware of the activities of the Union leaders whom he alleged for playing unclean hands with the Indian Congress without the knowledge of the Mizo people. However, the masses were over-intoxicated with enthusiasm at the thought of abolishing the Lushai chieftainship and could not see their political salvation; and thus they had to choose 'Baraba' in lieu of Jesus Christ.

The people rebelled over the political change to come, they unknowingly hoped, for their betterment. They could not reason anything other than the abolition of chieftainship, impressed coolie, etc., which unwittingly awed them disregarding any political reasoning. This had similarities with the Congress policy of abolishing the *zamindari* system and other landholdings in India. The Congress, then, and hands with the leaders of the Mizo Union drawing same line of propaganda against the British colonialism. This political unconsciousness of the people and the high intrigue of the Congress in sowing seeds of hatred of white people posed the Indian as a saviour of the Mizo people from the colonial yoke. The Union leaders were not even ashamed to lead the people in that way.

They imported the Gandhian way of non-violence movement and demonstrated how the movement works. I was a boy in 1948; I joined non-violence processionists who were to demonstrate in Lungleh. We were more than two thousands, one of the biggest procession, and we marched on towards the building of the administrative office and hotly shouted a slogan about a certain English administrator to go back to his country. As a matter of fact, he had to go back; that was certain. When I have grown up I asked my friends and older folks what was all about the procession and the slogan we enthusiastically shouted for, but none could give me reasonable answer. Really we were enthusiastic in 1948. We were ready to give anything for what our leaders pronounced a just cause and if they called for. Our procession was intercepted by police with lathi charged; many got injured. My tears was shed what I saw bloods spluttered on the face of the injured. We were then filled with intense dislike of the white people and those who were serving under them. Although there was no reason to hate the Britishers, but we were to do so because the Indians whom we never know before posed themselves as a saviour of the Mizo people from the colonial bondage.

The Mizo Union, having accepted the Indian enticement, submitted a memorandum on 22nd April, 1947, to the Government of India with the following demands:

With the National Council having the supreme legislative authority and executive body and judiciary within the district the composition and function of which will be prescribed by rules.

Any concurrence subjects in which the District (Mizo) may be connected with autonomous province of Assam or India as a whole shall be by negotiation with National Council which will be set up according to wishes of the general public; any legislation may be applied to the district only with the sanction of the Council with any modification.

Territorial unity and solidarity of the whole Mizo population to be known henceforth as Mizo and Mizoram for Lushai and Lushai Hills District, retaining the sole proprietory right over the land.

Special financial provision by the Centre from year to year until such time as the Mizo shall assert that they are able to maintain their territorial integrity and self-determination without this financial provision.

All the above items shall be subject to revision according to the future trend of events even to the extent of seceding after ten years.

In the course of five years after Indian Independence a District Council was offered and constituted in Mizoram in 1952. In the formation of the District Council the spirit and hope of the memorandum was fell dead. Yet, it was welcomed openly by the Union leaders no matter how limited the scope it opened towards the progress of the people. Because the provisions offered for a District Council in the Sixth Schedule of the Constitution of India were very much short of what has been demanded in the memorandum of 1947. Notwithstanding the fact that the Mizo Union leaders simply gave their acquiescence and remained unconcerned of the context of memorandum. On the other hand they tried to pacify the general public about the Indian offer of the District Council. They impressed the people to look forward to this Council as a temporary measures to the ladder of future progress. But, during the course of about fifteen years of the District Council administration in Mizoram it proved a useless tool for better progress and development. Now-a-days people consider it as colonialism in the name of democracy.

Another political party of the same time was United Mizo Freedom Organisation advocating integration with the Union of Burma. The Party has comparatively less control over the people. Moreover, the U.M.F.O. party stressed the need to maintain solidarity of the Mizo people with their brothers in the Chin Hills. The party leaders had talks with the Burmese leaders on this issue. Yet, the people who were affiliated to the majority party, the Mizo Union, were not impressed any farsighted political ideas of their leaders. They were not in a position to reason anything except the abolition of the Lushai chieftainship and soon the departure of the Britishers from the Lushai Hills whereby, they hoped for prosperity and happiness under the Indians. This state of their ecstacy overlapped all other political considerations. The U.M.F.O. seemed to have more sensible approach to the politics of the Mizo people for post-British colonial rule. They were not in favour of abolition of the chieftainship; nor they propagate hatred of the Britishers. They did not welcome, in anyway, overnight change after the British departure. They rather advocated continual change of the situation in Mizoram according to future trend of political aspiration of the Mizo people.

There was also a non-political group from elite circles with quite a number of followers. This group of people strongly advocated independence for Mizo people. They had a view that for best interest of the Mizo people it is necessary to maintain territorial integrity and solidarity of the whole Mizo people. They considered this preceded all other considerations of the nation's would be status after the British departure. They had a conviction that theirs is to seek a political freedom first and then, other things will be added unto it. Yet the majority party took up the country's undeveloped economic position for a propagative tool of their party's stand. Even a common salt came up a question on the political platform and people feared such independence of Mizoram without the common salt. The people of the majority party were whimsical about their own political doctrine, because the Congress had hands in it. The advocates of the independence of the Mizo people were on the other hand, pessimistic about a small Christian country's merger into a vast ocean of the Hindus. The patriotic view of the affair received sympathy from enlightened circle of the citizens that hoisting of Indian

National Flag at Aizawl had been delayed for fear of untowards incidents. At the same time, some sections wanted to retain relation with the British in the form of Crown colony. This seemed to have won the acceptance of the British officials and workers in Mizoram.

Under the circumstances the Mizo people were very young in politics and their way of thinking in the political affairs was immature. They felt their daily problems; they did think chiefs were a burden and they were suffered on account of the British domination; and free India would relief from all this. The majority party leaders had no political foresight on a national level and the Indian National Congress was a beacon light for their political considerations. They were not seeing the dynamic character of political ideas which shall also be true in the case of Mizo people. Indian Congress, taking the advantage of the affairs, reduced political virginity of the Mizo people and their political infancy was spoiled. Now, that the leaders of the majority party can see with their own eyes what they have committed for their own people only twenty years ago. Their children now are paying with lives and blood for what they had unconsciously done in 1947. Had India been sensible as the British in dealing this kind of affairs, such of the expense in lives and blood could have been saved. Political mistake is very costly and, therefore, one should think not only twice but a hundred times before he goes. Moreover, the price of freedom is too dear to be bought and its market is controlled by vested interests. If mankind is to inherit peace in the course of human generation these discrepancies should be abolished.

I wrote this book in October 1967 and revised it in March 1968. I made several modifications since my first intention was only for a supplement to 'MIZORAM'—about the struggle of Mizo people for freedom and building of the Mizo Nation, which I wrote in the middle of 1966. Deep gratitude is owed to Pu Lalkhawliana, Finance Minister of Mizoram for his untiring help which I benefited unboundedly. Credit should be given to him for some of the thoughts.

Lal Hmingthanga
Former MNF Foreign Minister

March 21, 1968
'LIBARTI'

Acknowledgements

In connection with this book I acknowledge with deep gratitude from my former underground friends for their help in getting this book, which has been once completely lost.

My very sincere acknowledgement is extended to Mr. H. Lallianmawia who helped me in computer-typing.

I gratefully acknowledge to Miss Lalhmachhuani, daughter of Pu Lal Hmingthanga for providing me her late father's photograph, and encouraging me in publishing this book.

At last but not the least I want to my thank to Rev. Dr. Zairema (RIP), one of the most respectable Church Ministers of the Mizos, for he willingly presented me his manuscript 'Mizo Problem' in 1983 and from whose manuscript I borrowed the idea and meaning of *Tlawmngaihna*. Rev. Dr. Zairema happened to be the father-in-law of Lal Hmingthanga.

Aizawl

Prof. J.V. Hluna
Editor

Contents

Introduction

The Mizos, like any other group of people who have lived together for several generations, have developed certain group peculiarities and unique characteristics. They think and react like most other orientals but they have certain traits which distinguish them from others. While it is impossible to describe these fully or while there is a danger in over-generalisation an attempt will nevertheless be made to introduce the socio-cultural life of the Mizos. So that the readers will be able to grasp the background of the book.

The then State of Assam was a land where races meet. The southern part of Assam Hills, extending to the Hill of Burma and Chittagong Hills in Pakistan, inhabited by a group of people often known as "The Lushai-Ku Ki" group. The people living in Mizo District were known as Lushai, whereas those scattered elsewhere are often grouped as "Kuki". Some of them live close to the Khasis and Nagas. Those who live close to Nagaland combine the characteristics of both Nagas and Lushai-Kuki group. The Lushai Kuki group have similar cultures, religious practices and speak similar language. They can understand each other. No doubt, they are descendant of common patriach, not far removed in history. It might have taken about five centuries to develop these differences in language and ways of living. As far as we know, one clan speaking one dialect would live together in one village; but through inter-marriage and other factors there were also cases when several clans lived together in different sections of the same village under one leader. There were often inter-clan quarrels so that one clan tended to cling together. Population pressure and inter-clan quarrels drove some of the more adventurous to move further away from their ancestral territories. In the present Mizoram, at the time the British came, there were living not less than 20 different clans who spoke different dialects. British administration brought inter-clan quarrels to a stop. The pioneer educations adopted the widest spoken dialect called "Duhlian" as the medium for production of literature and instruction in schools. At present, except in the borders of Bangladesh region only this language is spoken. The Hmars in Mizoram, for instance, have forgotten their dialect while this dialect is still going strong in the neighbouring State of Manipur and North Cachar in Assam. Even for a Mizo it is no longer possible to tell who belongs to which clan unless he has previous informations. In villages, people knew each other and the saying "blood is thicker than water" can still be felt as an under current among different clans. On marriage days, for example, a man may invite only a certain clan blood-relation to perform manual labour in preparing feasts. These people will feel neglected and insulted if they are not thus invited and they cannot refuse the invitation—it is their social obligation. Others may not be invited and even if they were invited they were not obliged to come.

Before the British period, the Chin-Lushai-Kuki group were semi-nomadic, moving from one village site to another. They never stayed in one place very long. They would cultivate a site once and move to another next year. If they could, they would like to have their *jhums* as close to the village as possible. Among other tribals, there is a definite landholding system but not among the Chin-Lushai-Kuki group. Practising shifting cultivation, they used to shift their homes also according to convenience. They do not care to undertake anything of permanent nature, like planting late yielding fruit trees. This has a profound influence on their character and psychology. Among them there was no division of labour, only two types of professionals were known, e.g., the blacksmith and the medicineman. These people did not even have enough customers to occupy them full-time, they performed their profession part-time. A man had, therefore, to be at once a cultivator, a warrior, a carpenter, a weaver, a hunter, etc. In other words, he had to be a jack of all trades and, therefore, it was not easy to be a master of one. They can be good at any job, better than, perhaps, average. In fact. Zairema said, "I have not met or seen any group of people so, ingenious and good at improvisation but rarely will you find anyone of them very good at one thing". To be good at anything, needs determination and patient doggedness which Mizos lack. This manifest in various forms.

A number of development schemes have been introduced in Mizoram by the Government of Assam and the present Government of Mizoram itself. Unlike many people of India who are mostly very conservative, Mizos will take them up with enthusiasm. Few people have the patience to carry the scheme through to a proper conclusion. It is not that they are unwilling to undertake something permanent and good for the future; but new ideas come that appear to involve less labour but to be more profitable and so they abandon the old and try their hand at the new. Fortunately this is still possible, because opportunities are plentiful. A time is bound to come when they will have to stick to one thing in order to succeed. This tendency to take new things enthusiastically but not to stick to them has been the cause of failure of many projects undertaken by the Mizos. The MNF leaders were well aware of this and had taken precautions accordingly. It is reported that a number of documents, such as lists of their membership had been camouflaged and to prevent them from surrendering or giving up after the novelty of the things had passed. When the general amnesty was proclaimed from time to time many MNF personnel surrendered and returned to normal life.

In the Mizo society a man has to produce for himself everything he needs. He has to learn all things and this creates a spirit of self-reliance. In some sense, therefore, the Mizos are most individualistic. There is a saying "*No khat ei theuh theuh*" which may be put thus—"All individuals eat the same one plate quantity of rice". One man eats one plate of rice, another eat the same quantity. In the Mizo philosophy the input is the same, the output should be the same. Therefore, what the one can do, the other also can do. In other words, they have the basic philosophy of life that one man is as good as the other. Mizos are not so foolish as to believe that all men are equal in strength wisdom or bravery; but they do believe that one man can be as strong, wise or brave as others. He is, therefore, prepared to attempt to do anything others can do.

In India, for example, the low-castes developed the fatalistic attitude that they are not, perhaps, as good as the high caste. Social conventions did not allow them to do many things that high castes did. This fortunately dying out, but a few years ago, they would not even attempt to better their lot in life. With encouragements from all sides, they have gone ahead and a number of them are now holding responsible and high positions. Even in these cases the instinctive complex feeling towards the high-castes is quite noticeable. They have tendency to hide their origin, and behave in a more vindictive manner with the Mizos, there is no such thing. A Mizo, however, unlettered or poor, does not have that type of feeling and, therefore, if he sees a violin, for example, he thinks he can play it and may actually try his hand. If he has something to say to the chief, he will go straight to him, without any saluting and say what he has to say. The British, who are perhaps the most formal nation practising protocol, etc., to the highest degree, when first came to the district they found this trait quite annoying. The missionaries, who were in charge of education, had to teach their pupils "manners". The Mizos have no word equivalent to greetings like *namaste*, *salaam* or good morning all in searching for a suitable word, they picked the word '*Chibai*' a word the priests used to call and greet the devils to act as the Mizo equivalent for these forms of greetings. Every morning, the school children had to say '*Chibai*' to the missionary who stationed himself at the gate. At first it was difficult but Mizos have no difficulty now in using their style cramped to use the word as an absolute term for show of respect in body posture of any form was not much practised. Speak to any Mizo, he is likely to reply without changing his original posture. Do not interpret this as rudeness done on purpose. Courtesy behaves to men in a similar manner. A Mizo woman will speak to anybody without feeling any sort of embarrassment, even to strangers. She may even move among a group of men, even cross or trample their legs without self-consciousness.

This individualism also shows in discipline. If you are as good as the other, he has no reason to order you about. But then, how was discipline maintained? This is not easy to explain that it was done by what we may call "example" method. The way a Mizo worrior maintained discipline is to take away the reasoning power of a man and make him an automat and India also adopted this doctrine. A number of Mizo boys enlisted in the Indian Army and Zairema remarked that to maintain discipline among them is not easy. No Mizo officer would be happy to command a battalion of Mizo boys at headquarters but he would be quite happy to do so on the war front. Leaders extract obedience from their men by the respect he evokes through his qualities. It is well known that among the MNF volunteers there were some great difficulty. They were not paid and perhaps have to manage for themselves for food and clothing. Their officers would find it exceeding difficult to command these untrained boys unless they themselves had exceptional qualities. So they did not perform well as an organised army unit; still they were proved formidable opponents in guerrilla warfare in several encounters. In order to teach a Mizo successfully, the teacher must be really good at his subject both in theory and practice.

This trait has some important consequences detrimental to themselves in modern life. The Cooperative Movement, for example, has been a complete failure among the Mizos. In other parts of India they have been successive and the failures are mostly due to inefficiency and corruption among the officials. Among the Mizo the prime cause of failure of such movements is the failure to cooperate. A farmer, for instance, instead of cooperating with other farmers to maintain price line would try to find the way most advantageous to himself. He is more concerned with his immediate needs and the pressure of the moment than the possible effect on others; not that the wishes to harm or to do anything bad to others.

In the old days, it was necessary for a Mizo to have more than his yearly needs; he would cultivate *jhum* industriously but if he had more than his need he would more likely let it not than keep extra pigs. This was not a simple case of laziness. A Mizo says, "*Hmeichhe finin tuikhur ral a kai lo*," while he thinks that he does not cross the valley it does not seem to go much beyond the next river. Elaborate planning of his failure is not in his nature.

He does not take easily to planting cash crops which may yield him income in some distant future; he would rather plant annually. Better communications and marketing facilities may change him more quickly than any efforts by the government to teach him.

In their fight for survival against nature Mizos and all primitive people had to develop this individualism. The need for survival against his enemies had taught him the necessity of having others about to help him. This has effect and counter-balanced the danger of extreme individualism. A Mizo developed a code of conduct calls *tlawmngaihna* which literally means "unwillingness to be defeated". This may seem a negative concept, but it expresses itself in a positive manner. If you do not want your enemy to defeat you, the only other alternative is to defeat him. So *tlawmngaihna* expresses itself in trying to defeat or beat others. In higher form of religion, the concept of God has a deep influence on the life and character of the believer. A believer tries to live upto the idea he has about the God he worships. Among the Mizos, his ideas of God have little influence on his daily conduct. His actions and springs of life are governed by this concept of his *tlawmngaihna*. This is his code of conduct that binds his society together, and it is that makes a Mizo prefer the company of his own people.

An Englishman will no doubt prefer the company of another Englishman to that of a Chinese, and here in India, a Punjabi will rather live with another Punjabi. Common language and culture draw people together and it is natural that it should be so. This *tlawmngaihna* is practised by all people throughout the world in one form or the other; among the Mizos it is practised and cultivated to a high degree in social relations. Among some nations one form of it may be highly developed but another side of it may be neglected. Among the Chinese or Japanese one of it is practised to a high degree in the concept of "face saving". Among others, it is practised in excessive forms of hospitality to their quests; among European in earlier days, it sometimes took the form of "gentlemen's honour". It covers thing like a sense of one's duty. Once a non-Mizo understands this concept and how it works among the Mizos, he enjoys their society. Since there is conscious attempts to practise this in all spheres of life, a Mizo, whatever may be his education or status in life, will always prefer the company of his fellow Mizos. In other Chin-Lushai-Kuki group scattered elsewhere, one noticeable thing among their practices is their preference to live in small villages. Among the Mizos, the villages are generally large, not such less than 100 families. Individualism tends to break up, but *tlawmngaihna* binds together. Zairema believed that among the other Lushai-Kuki groups this had not developed along the same lines or to the same degree as it has among the people in Mizoram.

The underlying principle of *tlawmngaihna* is the spirit of this unwillingness to be defeated. No nation, it is true, will undertake a war to be defeated; no sportsman will enter a competition to be beaten. In the same manner, a Mizo will try his best to be "undefeated" in the practice of any social duties, demands and standards. In one way it is a form of self-glorification, not at all irritating to others but most pleasant to encounter. A Mizo tries to outshine his friends and in so doing may have to undergo all sports of hardships. For example, it is the duty of the young people to dig graves when there is death. Every youngmen will try to be the first to get to the grave and do the largest amount of work. If there is an errand to be run, he will try to perform the most difficult and arduous jobs. He will appear to enjoy the domestic work of the bereaved family although it is much more enjoyable to go out hunting. At night he will choose the most dangerous and the least comfortable spot in the camp for his sleeping place. He will always think of the comfort of others and their convenience before him.

The story of a valiant and unselfish man, *Taitesena* had been told over and over again and every Mizo child knows it by heart. This young man is put up as a role model for boys to follow. He seemed to have some sort of morbid obsession that he would not live long and, therefore, he would not go out with his friends to woo the girls in the evening according to the usual custom. He would prefer to remain behind at *zawlbuk* where men of the village would come together for gossip. The men used to send the young boys on errands and at night in the dark, for the very young boys this could be dangerous. When any man tried to send small boys to do any errand, this man would immediately jump up and offer his services and shamed others by this *tlawmngaihna*. In his presence no man would ill treat anyone or send small boys on errand. His *tlawmngaihna* was seen one day when they were re-roofing *zawlbuk*. A cold wind and rain forced all others to get down and take shelter. He refused to come down but continued his work in spite of the rain. This might be considered foolishness and unnecessary exposure to pain and suffering, but it was his *tlawmngaihna* that drove him to do it and people would admired him for it. Once on a hunting party they camped at a spot where nothing was available and they had to eat their rice dinner without any curry. One of the elders found it difficult to eat and said, "How foolish we are; if we had the sense to take that *tumbu* (wild plaintain flower) we saw at noon today, we would have enjoyed our dinner". When they got up next morning, they found *Taitesena* cooking. While they slept, he had gone to bring the *tumbu* and cooked it for their morning meal. On another occasion, one of their elders, while crossing a stream, found a stone quite suitable and good for *lungtat* (a grindstone) exactly to his fancy. He said, "I wish I could take it home". Later on, when they got home, *Taitesena* approached the man and said to him, "Sir, here is your *lungtat*". In an attempt to save the lives of his friends, he was killed by a wounded tiger.

Tlawmngaihna is expressed at times in ways which may seem quite foolish to non-Mizos. It is a custom to carry a dead body home if the relatives wish it so. All the young men would come out and carry the body. One might think that if a dozen or so of them carry the body and the rest go back to their work to take their turn next time, it would save much wasted labour. A Mizo does not look at it that way. All the young people will come out and each will try to be the one who carries for the longest distance. The young men of the next village will meet them at a recognised boundary; instead of just handing the corpse over the former will try to carry it across the territory of the other village. It is a matter of *tlawmngaihna* for the other village, to prevent the other village to carry more than their share and so there would be much pushing and pulling to take over. This is known as *mizawn inchuh*. Sometimes quarrels also arose, but all this being done as a matter of *tlawmngaihna* it was never serious. Injuries like cuts, bruises and even broken ribs were forgiven in a congenial mood.

Among the Orientals it is a matter of etiquette if your host offers you more food then you should refuse it. If he is a good host he will give you more in any case knowing that you have not enough yet. This is also covered by *tlawmngaihna* in a peculiar form. If anyone comes to your place while you are eating you must offer him what you are eating; but the other party must refuse. For the non-Mizos it may be difficult to know how to behave in such circumstances for fear of offending the host. If a low caste man in India, offers you something to eat and if you refuse it, he may think that you have refused the food because he is a low caste and perhaps feels insulted too. Since there is no such feeling among the Mizos, you will not offend their feelings by refusing anything they offer you to drink or eat. So refuse it like any other good Mizos would do. However, the Mizos may apologize first by saying that they are poor and that they have nothing good to offer, etc., then you have to accept. A Mizo will also refuse an invitation to a feast unless the host is a very near relative; no offence is intended because the invitee refuses to go since he does not want to put the host to any inconvenience.

Even he accepts he will eat as little as possible and try to be the first to finish the meal. When sitting at a feast or any meal it is not 'ladies first' among Mizos it is the 'eldest first'. It was a custom to honour the youngmen who showed the most *tlawmngaihna* by giving him the first cup of rice-beer on certain feast days. Every young would try to receive this honour, but at the time of receiving, if he was too eager,.he would lose his reputation. He would hide himself; but unless and until he had his cup, the feast could not start. Others would search for him and drag him forcibly to receive the honour.

It is in the sphere of helping others in need that *tlawmngaihna* shows its nobleness. In case of sickness in a family, others will come to help in nursing the sick. If the case is serious, the whole house may be full of people ready to do anything to help. Day and night they will be there and finally, death comes, the young people will run errands to inform relatives living as far as a day's journey away. The house will be full of people bringing them some gifts, and for a week or so they will not leave the bereaved family to bear their grief alone. They may make jokes, sing songs together or just talk in order to divert the minds of the bereaved. At least for a fortnight, young men will sleep in that house always ready to do anything to help the family. This is somewhat difficult for non-Mizos to understand. Some people prefer privacy to bear their grief alone. Among the Mizos this is not so and L.B. Thanga told me he found a number of non-Mizos who enjoy this form of *tlawmngaihna*.

During winter, spring water often dries up or the water decreases. In such cases, it was recognised that first-come should be served first. Drawing water is a specific duty of women and a number of them would gather to wait for their turn. If a man comes to draw water, the women immediately understand that all the women of that family have fallen ill and, therefore, they will give way at once to the man. Later on, they will take one pot of water and put it in the house of the family. Pounding and shifting of rice is also a woman's duty and so the neighbouring women would come and do the job for the family.

Tlawmngaihna, though basically selfish, works out in the most selfless actions. The most *tlawmngai* people are not only those who try to outshine their friends in performing all kinds of services, but also those who show the greatest desire to inflict as little pain or inconvenience on others in any form or manner. A sick man will not groan but try to make light of it as much as possible.

This is to draw least sympathy from others. He knows that it is not enjoyable to sit near a sick man who groans or cries. The story of a man, *Neuva* will illustrate this point. In trying to save the life of his friend from a wounded tiger, this man received a fatal wound. The tiger hit him on the neck. Somehow, he managed to hold up his head with his hands. His friends, seeing that he was seriously injured tried to carry him home on a stretcher. He refused completely saying that he could walk very well. He, however, requested one of his friends to hold his hand. When they got home, he took his seat on the verandah and called for his *vaibel* (smoking pipe). When it was brought he had three puffs and then removed his hands which hold his head up. The head came lolling down and he died immediately. His neck bone had been broken.

You can do almost anything among the Mizos by appealing to their *tlawmngaihna* if done at the right moment in the right manner.

It will not be complete unless something of the position of women is mentioned. While the chief role of a woman is found at home, she is not confined to domestic duties alone. She has also to do all the jobs men have to do for their livelihood. Besides the usual domestic duties she is responsible for making clothes for herself and the family. A man has to pay for his wife, in the old days, in terms of domestic *mithuns*. The price of a bride depends on several considerations—the custom of her clan, her industry, her chastity and her beauty. A virgin girl may bring as much as five *mithuns*, but if she is not a virgin she may bring much less. For this reason a girl has to be careful. The cost of a *mithun* was formally fixed at Rs. 20 but today, the old reckoning is abandoned and bride prices ranges from Rs. 400 to Rs. 500 in cash. Dating a girl is not practised as in the West, but it is done by mutual agreement. A girl cannot do as much work as a boy; but a boy and a girl or a group of them will agree to date each other in this way—they will work in their *jhums* by turn. The girls will look after the work—to dry the wet clothes of their children, wash them if dirty, and repair them if torn. In this way a boy and a girl may date each other for three years before they decide to get married. Today things are changing, they may get married even before a month elapsed.

Women are free to mix with the men but they may not go to *zawlbuk* (the bachelor quarters). She may speak to a stranger and a good woman in fact will try to make even strangers feel at home. She takes pride in hard working. The wife of a high ranking Mizo official will never think of taking a servant to carry her purchases from a market. A Mizo woman never takes a holiday till death forces her to do so. Discipline for her is strict, and she starts working from the age of six or seven by taking charge of the baby when her mother had to go to her work. The only pleasure Mizo women enjoy fully without lot or hindrance is to make beautiful designs for clothes. A man may divorce his wife for any reason or even without any reason. She does not hold property. If her husband dies, all the family property goes to the husband's nearest relative. She has only one cane basket where she may put her personal clothes and this is the only property she can say is her own. Wife beating was common, but women rarely fought back. Poligamy was rare, but practiced. The men found it better to have one wife.

Mizoram was formally brought under British administration on 5th September, 1895. Since then the people have turned to paths of peace and made considerable progress in all spheres of life. Except for communication difficulties, it was a country where widows or orphans never lacked helping hands. Even the poorest could bury their dead in their own homes by merely expressing the wish, though this might involve four or five days journey. No dacoit party ever existed nor locks adored the doors of villages. Even the so-called criminals were so faithful and honest that their guards could leave them alone in jungles to collect firewood while they enjoyed themselves in teashops drinking or gossiping. There was actually a case when a guard so drunk that the companions of the guard had to carry him home and made false excuses for him to his superiors. 96 per cent of the people professed Christianity and have given up their old values completely. They are now fired with new ideals. The Christian teaching of universal brotherhood of men, as children of the same father God, has gripped their imagination and a number of them have left the comforts of their own homes and the society of their own friends to help uplift their less fortunate brothers in their hunting and practice of inhuman cruelty to their neighbouring people due to boundary disputes; and so there never was any serious disturbance of peace in the country. There had been political movements, protests, quarrels, etc., but none so grave as to cause serious damage to property or loss of life and calling for the use of arms to restore law and order. Not before 1966, in the whole history of administration was it necessary to impose curfew on the citizen. How is then such a peace loving people so suddenly rose up in arms against the Government of India under which they have enjoyed so much more freedom and privileges than any other Indian citizen? What made the professed followers of the Prince of Peace to resort to such widespread acts of violence? What were the factors that promoted the rapid growth of the Mizo National Front (MNF) party, which within three years of its existence, could capture two-third of the M.L.A. seats for the then Mizo District in the Assam State Legislature and in five years could gain enough support and smuggled arms from foreign sources to stage a revolt against the armed might of India? Political, socio-economic and psycho-religious questions are involved and an attempt was made. Lal Hmingthanga, former MNF Foreign Secretary, in this book to answer these questions and assessed the situation. And at the same time, several agencies handed their hands to bring peaceful solution of the Mizo uprising. The question of peace making problems is also assessed from one's view and the other.

This book entitled *Problem of Peace-Making in Mizoram* was written by Lal Hmingthanga, the underground MNF Foreign Minister and was published in *Dampa Weekly* in February 1969. It was reported that it had been banned and burnt down at the order of the Government before it was formally released. Its contents are purely the ideology and political thought of the author during the Freedom Struggle of MNF. Since the MNF and the Government of India concluded peace, all underground personnnel returned to normal life in one of the Indian States—Mizoram—the issues and ideas of the writer of this book may not be relevant and may be controversial in today's political scene. However, history is history, it records the facts and events. This book also has a historical value in Mizo History in general and the MNF movement in particular, and I decided to edit and publish it for the students as well as researchers in this field.

J.V. Hluna
Editor

REFERENCES

Census of India 1901 by B.C. Allen, B.A., I.C.S., Superintendent of Census Operation, Assam.

Church and Political Upheaval in Mizoram by John Vanlal Hluna, Mizo History Association, 1985.

NOTE: On the Lushais by Major Shakepeare, C.I.E., D.S.O., Superintendent of the Lushai Hills.

The Mizo Identity and the Mizoram by L.B. Thanga, I.A.S. (Rtd.) in the International Seminar on the studies on the minority nationalities of North-East India—THE MIZO.

Unpublished manuscript of Zairema on Mizo Problem handed over to the Editor by Rev. Zairema himself in 1983.

1

Mizo : A Deprived Nation

Mizo belongs to the Mongolian race of Tibeto-Burman stock migrating from the Southern part of China to their present habitat of land; bordered by Burma on the East, India on the North, and Pakistan on the West. They are a numerous families of clans closely knitted together by common traditions, customs, culture, mode of living, language and rites. Being a numerous family of clans, they are wrongly identified by their neighbouring States by calling different names such as Kukis, Lushai, Chins, Arrakanese, etc. However, the solidarity of the Mizo people as a nation stands unshakable.

Mizo have a free society where men and women, boys and girls work, meet, sing and dance together on special occasions. Their cultural affinity is towards Burmese, Thais, Indonesians and Philippines. Their religion before introduction of Christianity was animism. The Mizo are, up to this day, completely differ from Indians, Burmese and Pakistanese, in matter of religious practices, culture, social life and ideology. For the Mizo, to assimilate with Indians, Burmese and Pakistanese is like an attempt to weld iron and clay together.

The Mizo had never been under foreign domination before the British interference during the last two decades of the nineteenth century. Mizoram was subsequently brought under the British Political control. For the sole purpose of administrative convenience, the British Government divided the Mizo country into three divisions, without obtaining the will and consent of the people. When the British granted Independence to India, Burma and Pakistan, the British Administrative boundaries falling within Mizoram becomes an International boundary between Burma and India without the knowledge of the Mizo Nation.

When Mizoram was divided international boundaries between India and Burma falls at the very heart of Mizoram. These man-made boundaries served as a barrier for political, social and economic progresses affecting the whole Mizo Nation. No political movement of Mizo could cross the international boundaries. In spite of such hope, less vivisections, the minds, the thoughts and the social life of Mizo remained unchanged wherever they were. The general feelings of Mizo nationals in India was the feeling of being unwanted, despised and alien. Meanwhile, no Mizo worker felt secure under an Indian boss; no student felt favoured by Indian masters, and no Mizo soldier in the Indian Armed Forces felt that he was fighting for his country.

The more a Mizo has contact with an Indian, the more he feels lonesome alien unwanted. A Mizo works in the Indian Government Services not because he is aware of Indian call but only because of his needs to earn for a living. When undeclared war broke out between China and India or India and Pakistan, an ordinary Mizo would say "India is fighting against China or against Pakistan", and never say, "We are fighting against China or against Pakistan", A Mizo never includes himself in what anything India is doing. He looks India as a foreign country nor as his. In the minds of a Mizo, India, Ceylon, Burma or Pakistan are all the same except that India imposes more authority over him. This feeling is prevalent not only among Mizo within India but also within Burma and Pakistan. It is, therefore, quite clear that no Mizo can be moulded with foreigners inasmuch as a piece of clay cannot be moulded with iron. Some day, some time, they shall surely fall apart.

Though Mizoram has been vivisected, Mizo as a Nation has the right to self-determination wherever they are, form their Government, rule themselves and mould their life in their own chosen way like any nation of the world. This is the undeniable rights endowed by our Creator and affirmed by the United Nations Charter. No Indians, Burmese or any other nation can spoil this right. To unify all these vivisected areas into a single compact unit again and attain national status for themselves among the family of nations is, therefore, the sacred duty for every Mizo wherever he or she is. It is to this and that Mizoram is working and will struggle till all the rights are fully restored.

In respect of the carved out Mizoram falling within Indian domination, the leading citizens reserved the right of secession from India after ten years from attainment of the Indian Independence. A memorandum affecting to this right was submitted to the then Government of British India. After experiencing fifteen years of Indian rule, the

Mizo people have decided to claim their rights and run their future in their own way. Independence movement was accordingly come into being. All possible efforts to have smooth and peaceful restoration of this right had been made with Indian leaders. On every occasion the Mizo leaders astoundingly proved the rights of deciding their own future so much so that the Indian leaders and officials were dumbfounded. On realization of failure in those arguments the Indian leaders simply turn deaf ears to those realities.

2

We are Compelled to Resist

When India found that she could not stamp out the rights of the Mizo people on the table, she mobilized her armed strength to achieve what she has failed through arguments and persuasion. Accordingly, the Government of India installed more military posts inside Mizoram, strengthened the existing posts and stationed her most modern military might on the very border of Mizoram to enable them move in a moment notice. The Mizo leaders immediately protested against the military build-up as the Indian intention and its result could clearly be visualized. Even at that stage the Indian leaders turned deaf ears and refused to have any discussion on this matter.

The picture of the Government of India's intention and their long drawn preparation of military suppression over the Mizo people was taking shape on war footings during the month of February 1966. Therefore, we had been driven into a situation which was much against our will. Leaders and patriots of the Mizo Nation in their mass meetings decided and avowed that they shall never submit to force however strong it may be, and are determined to defend their country, their beloved Mizoram, with every possible means. Meanwhile, they appealed to the Supreme Judge of the World for rectitude of their intention and to all the peace loving nations to make effort for bringing about peace in Mizoram in accordance with the stipulation of the Fundamental of Human Rights.

While the country was in a state of explosive situation, as a result of Indian Military treachery, the Indian troop with arms surrounded the Mizo National Front General Headquarters at Aizawl while a prayer meeting was held inside. All the inmates were arrested, the Holy *Bible* and hymn books of Christian were seized and burnt. One Block officer of the MNF party was shot dead in jail without exercising any justice to him. Others were tortured and manhandled and some of them were murdered. We were forced into a situation where we cannot remain idle watching our friends being mercilessly persecuted and tortured in our soil by the Indians solely on reasons of our rights and dignity as human person.

The Sacred Call of the Nation to safeguard her National Integrity and the will of the people was made all over the country. In order to defend the Rights and Dignity of the Mizo Nation—Representatives of the Mizo people declared Independence of Mizoram State on the First of March, 1966.

The whole populace of Mizoram irrespective of their political affiliations declared their support and loyalty to the newly formed Government of Mizoram and affirmed their willingness and determination to uphold their rights till freedom is won with peace and tranquillity in the country.

The First day of March, 1966 was a turning point in the history of the Mizo people. We, then decided to disarm the Indian troops stationed in our land. That was purely a measure which would demonstrate our strong protest against the military suppressive policy of the Government of India over the people of Mizoram. Action was strictly controlled so that it might not escalate into a larger conflagration. Much restrain was used when the movement was started with the last word said by the Operation Commander, "Save life whether Mizo or Indian". Meanwhile we firmly declared that we will yield in no way to the disposition of Indian Military suppression, and we will uphold the truth of our rights to self-determination, that is if Mizos are to live they shall live as a nation. There can be no side tract or half way.

Our intention was not to kill the Indian soldiers at random; except in self-defence, but only to convince them that we were fighting for the nation's freedom and we have no hatred against them (grudge towards them). What we want was their understanding of our stand and if they could surrender with their arms to the Commanding Officer of the National Volunteers, no action would be directed against them. They were also told that it is the duty of every honest person to jointly stand against wrong and to stand together for the right and dignity of mankind and to seek justice for maintaining lasting peace which is the duty of every sane person. Understanding this some of the Indian military personnel surrendered with their arms to the Volunteers without any conflict. But, unfortunately, some of the Indian Army Commanders resorted to shooting of the National Volunteers. This then resulted into bitter conflicts between the National Volunteers and the Indian Army at some places.

3

Indian Troops Reinforcement

While the resistance movement of disarming the Indian Armed personnel was in progress, a Division of the Indian troops, with the support of the Mountain Battery moved into our territory. Their Air Force provided them with air cover by strafing and clearing all obstructions along the road leading from Silchar to Aizawl. Being the commercial line of Mizoram numerous villages are situated all along the road. These villages became the obvious target of the Indian Jet Fighters which strafed without discriminating civilian populations. Their 25 Pounder Guns blew up long range targets of civilian hideouts who took shelter on the outskirt of the villages. On 5th and 6th March, the capital Aizawl was attacked by four Jet Fighters with bombs. Its main market and other central areas of Aizawl turned into ashes.

Meanwhile, the Government of Mizoram, issued an order to the National Volunteers not to resist the incoming Indian troops. All the Indian Military posts that had surrendered and were occupied by the National Volunteers were evacuated and Indian troops reoccupied them without meeting any resistance. This clearly indicated that we disfavoured an armed conflict for the settlement of our political demand, and in case if the situation demands it, we shall do everything according to our political necessity.

Unfortunately, without responding the measure taken by the Government of Mizoram to avoid armed conflict Government of India continued her suppressive measures towards the Mizo people. The Indian troops proceeded to village after village by killing, looting, arresting and torturing the civilian populations, almost all the villages where they can lay their hands were burnt down to ashes. The womenfolk, from minor girls of ten years to the old were raped at gun point in public, and some of them to death. No male adults can take care of his family or cultivation. They have all been, forced to work for the Indian soldiers without any food or reward.

The Indian troops have uprooted a number of villages from their native homes in their concentration camps where all able bodied workers have to work from dawn to dusk, paying them with a handful of food just sufficient to make them alive. The pity is that these unfortunate people were allowed to carry whatever they could on their shoulders at a time. Their fate is pitiable and of slavery. The number of Mizos in the concentration camps is over 60,000 persons. The fate of those who have not been uprooted is not enviable either. Indian troops demanded free labour from every able bodied workers. It is estimated that one man day is given by per week by all able bodied workers in Mizoram. To add to these hardships, whenever Indian troops, who were normally moving in company strength from village to village came to a village, the whole village has to be curfewed as long as they stay which lasted from two days to a week. In this way ordinary civilian life is now being harassed to an intolerable situation The people cannot work more than three days in a week in their daily task. Under these circumstances there is nothing but hunger and starvation for them. We are sure that it is the intention of India to starve all Mizos to death. Can there be anything as inhuman as that. They have outdevilled the Devil himself.

Whenever the Indian Army goes they occupy churches, robbing its properties and destroying what is left of them. People are tortured and shot even inside the churches. Priests have to hide themselves from the military brutality and imprisonment. Wherever a Hymns Book or *Bible* is found, they tear it to pieces and burnt it to ashes. The Mizo people are challenged in the very name of Christianity. The public prayer continually conducted, day and night, to their living God for the salvation from the Indian's beastly brutalities.

4

India Built Concentration Camps in Mizoram

Ever since March 1966, the people of Mizoram are struggling against the Indian armed suppression of their rights to national self-determination. In spite of all the nefarious activities and atrocities committed by the Indian Government rulers upon the Mizo people, their national solidarity and determination for the realization for their cherished goal remains unshattered. The last Indian General Election which was compulsorily imposed upon the Mizo people with a view to demonstrate the Indian Supreme rule over Mizoram was totally a failure. The people successfully resisted voting in the Indian poll 1967 and did not cast vote in spite of the threat of the Indian Forces to cast vote.

India, now drew more wicked line of oppressive tactic. Her surreptitious design to destroy the Mizo Nationalists and their fight for the right of self-determination was again taken shape and implemented by the hosts of her army during the month of January and February 1967. The operation is captioned "Operation Security" under which the Indian troops worked for the so-called Grouping, which is, in fact, the same as the German Concentration camps for Jews.

Life in the Grouping Centres

The manner by which the Indian troops carried out this plan was cruel and treacherous. The Indian troops in battle dress marched in the night and surrounded villages before dawn to make sure that no villager was escaped. The people were forced out of their ancestral homes with what they could carry in their hands. That was the last moment for them to have been in the fondest place of their hearts, their homes. They were then driven like cattle to where nothing, but only torture awaits them. The villages were set on fire by the human-cattle drivers, the Indian troops, while the people were still watching with rain of tears in their innocent faces. These are the villages they belong to from their great grand grandfathers down to their children and the only fondest place where their hearts belong to. Now it was destroyed and was nothing but ashes. "Oh Memories, I hate memories", cried out one woman desperately. In 1967, alone more than 60,000 people were uprooted from their ancestral homes and villages with all their goods and properties burnt down. The Indian troops, after the houses were vacated, searched the houses and had taken away any valuable they found and then destroyed with fire. The Indian regular troops, then with a booty of their plunder, drove away the people to where their unknown destiny lies. All the relics of their fore-fathers and the properties they have so laboriously earned and accumulated through years were totally burnt off. Their stores of grains and barns were also burnt, as the Government of India thinks that starvation of the Mizo people will be one of the effective instruments to crush the MNF movement.

The Grouping centres were at the beginning open fields, without, not to speak of housing facility, even shade. The inmates have had to lie down on the open field for days and nights. Children, even small babies, suffered under the scorching heat of the day and the chilly cold of the night, while their parents were building thatched huts. Over and above, the people were given meagre subsistence ration while the troops were engaged in a systematic programme of destruction. The grain stores which the village folk accumulated through the hard toil of the past years were the obvious target of their destructive activities. Hundred of barns were destroyed in a single day with fire, while the inmates of the camps were starving.

The living condition of the people in the Concentration Camp was miserable. As they were not provided with housing facility, all the reconstruction was to be born by themselves. Every of their movements was under strict vigilance of the troops and one pretext of suspicion has to be paid by life. As such, at Thingsulthliah Camp, three boys who were gone into the jungle to cut bamboos for their house were shot dead by the Indian soldiers on mere pretext. Their bodies were covered with leaves and left at the spot. Their relatives, conscious of their unusual absence, went to the place and found their bodies. Hence, the inmates of the camps were pitiful animals under the Indian watch-dogs.

The whole population of the concentration camps were poorly fed. Only very low subsistence were given to them. India as a whole is a starving country and it is understandable from the circumstances that no surplus food will be available for the extra Mizo people. If so, "why the Government of India destroyed foodgrains in Mizoram" is the question to be answered before the candid world. Does the Indian rulers really mean to annihilate the Mizo people or does it really hope to succeed its design of wiping out of the existence of more than half a million Mizos in India? God forbid. No power on earth will ever destroy the rightful existence of the Mizo people and their rights of self-determination. But, at the time, it is the selfish nation and it is the imperfect concept of the rulers of the Nation under which the Mizo people suffered yet. As the Mizo people are hard working their average consumption of food is high. Generally grown up person is supposed to consume one kilogram of rice in one day. The inmates of the concentration camps were given 1½ kilogram of rice together with 1½ kilogram of atta (flour) per head for a week ration. The hungry children were crying for food and it was an intolerable scene for parents to see their children unconscious of their oppressors' atrocities. It may be correct to say that to the oppressors, success is measured according to the degrees of the suffering of the people; the more miserable they are, the Indian masters count more success of their Operation Security.

During two decades of the Indian Government rule in Mizoram there has been only one dry season motorable road that links Silchar of Cachar District of India from the Southern terminus at Lungleh. Half section of the road from Lungleh to Aizawl was originally constructed by the voluntary service of the people between 1951 and 1954, the maintenance of which is later taken up by the Government of India. This same road, being very strategically important without which the Indian Government could hardly suppress the Mizo people of their rights and political aspiration, is now under improvement and costruction by the Indian military road builder, Border Road Task Force under a beautifully named "Special Development Scheme of Mizoram". But the real purpose of the Government is contrary. In fact, it is not for the development, but for the destruction. Swamp Army of cruel Indians are operating from this base and are working to do mostly ruins to the Mizo people by torturing the innocent people killing men and women at a simple pretext, plundering their properties, raping women and girls of under age, and many other nefarious deeds committed upon the innocent persons backup by the terrors of the guns' reign. Even sacred places and churches are molested by encamping themselves as their barrack. How happy Mizo would be, if India quit Mizoram and withdraw all her development schemes.

The Grouping Centres were also used as force labour camps. All the able persons were requisitioned to work in the military road construction and fencing work of the centres with strict regimentation. They were forced to work as and according to the labour supervisors' dictation. If a man raises any complaint he is paid slash of the armed supervisors whip. Normally a Mizo feels displeasure to perform unskilled work of road construction, unless it pays high enough, as he considers such nature of work below all the unskilled labourers were imported from India. Therefore, even the very nature of the work greatly harms their personal dignity and honour.

Further, the economic life of the Mizo people was greatly hampered by the Indian suppressive measures. *Jhuming* cultivation is the mainstay of the people, because there is no other wayout and is the only way opened for the masses under the Indian administration. The people could not pursue their normal duty of their *jhuming* works as they were not allowed to go out of the Centre. Moreover, the Security Force imposed forced labour and occasionally made calls to them for various works such as clearing of jungles along roads, fencing their camps and making bunker for them and carrying supplies and ammunitions for them. Sometimes, the civilians were taken by the Indian soldiers as a protection from surprised attack of Mizo National Front (MNF). And it always happened that in their patrolling post, the civilians were used for human-bunkers as a protection from the Mizo Army. For all these and other various harassments from the occupation army, the people were greatly hampered in their pursuit to keep on their living. The inmates of the Grouping Camps, in particular, were totally debarred from their *jhuming* cultivation. This inevitably caused total starvation to the people, which as mentioned before, was a means to force the people to rely on the oppressors' hands (this is called FCI supplies in today's coinage) till today. Consequently, their future is dimmed and their destiny is unknown in the wide-open mouth of Hell, India.

Thus, the appeal of the Mizo people to friends and humanities to God-fearing people and freedom loving nations is not to let them down into the mouth of the Hell; rather, to save them and to feed them till the days of this devil end. On the other hand, they are determined to fight on till peace prevails over their country with justice and honour maintained for all.

5

Reunification of the Mizo People 1968

History of the Mizo people living in the hills and plain areas between India on the west and Burma on the east in the Southern-East of Asian region is a history of domination by foreign rules. In the late nineteenth century, the British came to this Region of South-East Asia. Mizoram (at this time Mizoram had no name) is a mountainous region with a few plains here and there mostly along river valleys. The British could penetrate in this mountainous region only after strongly colonizing India and Burma. When the British came in expedition, the rulers of the land put up nominal resistance and they were easily defeated because the resistance was unorganized and tribal in manner.

The Mizo people, in spite of their common national identity, had no common nomenclature and their area of habitation was not legally defined. Mr. Grierson, compiler and publisher of Linguistic Survey of India had called the people Kuki-Chin Group and thoroughly investigated in which he stated that the people having such common national identity were inhabiting an area whose border was reaching as far as Miyttha River in the east and as far north bordering Nagaland. This people, with a political consciousness and realization of their neighbourhood called themselves in this late Twentieth Century Mizo (or Zomi).

When the British came, there was no international boundary dividing peoples of different nationalities except those defined and ruled by Kings, Rajas and Chiefs. Even these kingdoms and borders were subject to changes as a result of tribal wars. Therefore, there were no defined boundary between India and Burma; neither between Mizoram and India nor Mizoram and Burma. The British, for the purpose of their administrative convenience, divided Mizoram into two, and thus, the eastern part goes under the Burma colonial rule and the western portion under the colonial rule of India. Thus, the present conflicts between the people of Mizoram and Indian Government and that of the Government of Burma is a direct result of the careless deeds of the British Government hundred years ago.

In 1947 beginning the retreat of the British rule in Asia and as a result the Independence of India and Burma the Mizo people were left without any political arrangement. The people, as they were politically unconscious, were embarrassed and confused with the new political situation. The people were not aware of the political changes which vitally concerns their national interests, neither freedom nor rights in the sense of the terms. They could not even realized the Principles of Atlantic Charters whereby their rights of freedom were ensured by the Allied powers. Taking by this ignorance, India and Burma shared Mizoram between themselves as their rightful inheritance without giving any regard for the Rights of the People. This trouble colonialism cause the Mizo people great harm and the dignity of their nation stamped under foot. As a result progress of their civilization is hampered and their economics is only a system of total slavery.

Ever since the year 1947, politicians and some intellectuals of the Mizo people have felt the pang of colonial domination, and the injustice of their being separated by the colonial rules of Burma and India. They have well understood that these alien rules are against the Universal Human Rights. Mizo Union, (i.e., within India) in 1947, submitted a memorandum to the British India Government as well demanding the former to grant a political status, so that they would be able to frame up their future politics in respect of the Reunification of the Mizo people in Burma and India. Also in Chin Hills of Burma, a political party under the name of Chin National Organisation was set up in 1953 with an objective for the Reunification of all Chin (Mizo) people. Paihte National Council, a political party within the Indian rule, too, submitted to the Government of India a memorandum demanding freedom of the Mizo People with a chance to their reunification with their brother in Burma.

Reaffirming this principle and in support of the Reunification programme for Unity and National solidarity of all the Mizo people and for freedom, a political party within the Indian rule, the Mizo National Front in its memorandum of 1965, made appeal to the Government of India to grant right of self-determination for the Mizo people as already stated in Memorandum of the Mizo leaders in 1947. Zomi National Liberation Front of Burma, with the same objective in view came into being in 1967 and is fighting for freedom of the Zomi people against the rule of Burma. Besides, efforts of a number of enthusiastic individuals for the same cause cannot be left out. It is, therefore, crystal clear that, sooner or later, the reunification of all the Mizo people in India and Burma is a historical eminence and the only political goal of the Mizo people for freedom and solidarity of their Nation.

Having such national objective in view, the Mizo National Front in 1966, constituted an independent Government of Mizoram and had shaken off their relation with India on March 1, 1966. Similarly, the Zomi (Mizo) people in Burma followed suit and had shaken of their relation with Burma on June 1, 1968. Now, therefore, all the Mizo people are united in One Body-One Nation.

Consequence upon the Reunification of the Mizo people, a new history has born on which the future history is founded; the present generation is, thus charged with great responsibility to bear. In other words, a new chapter is opened in our history which thus put us to stand at an important juncture of two histories of the past and the future. Our present struggle has justified the old history and will also tell upon the future. Moreover, the following points may be stated with which the people of Mizoram is pursuing its policy of Nation Building.

1. By such Reunification respect and prestige to the Mizo people will be enhanced among families of

nations and the people of the world. Such unity secures more than one and a half millions of people united into force which affirms the national stand of the people. The colonialists, India and Burma, have despicably labelled us 'Tribal' which restrains foreigners to see the truth. This is a landmark which will demonstrate before the world the incredible calling and injustice done to the Mizo people. Besides, Burma and India can no longer conceal the fact that they are suppressing the rights of Mizo people.

2. Consequently, this Reunification will go a long way towards improvements of our relations and understandings with friendly countries. In spite of the fact that freedom is the right of nations, we have been meeting difficulties inasmuch as the evil design of the colonialists. We, thus, need helps of our friendly countries. To secure this help, we must ourselves, unite for it.

In this affair, powers and international boundary can not be respected. Whatever may help separation of Mizo people is wrong and is due to be resisted by any means. Whatever hinders our Reunification is due to be fought at any cost. We have no alternative but to fight for our just rights. What other people want we too want. What other nation cherish we too cherish. Therefore, we have no intention of ceasing our struggle unless this sacred duty is fulfilled, bringing all Mizos under one administration as a nation to take her rightful place in the family of nations.

Finally, from the facts stated above, it can clearly be summed up that Mizos shall not rest peacefully unless the undermentioned national objectives are fully achieved:

(i) That we may inherit our share of rights under the sun.
(ii) That we may free never to bow down again under the colonial rule.
(iii) That we may establish friendship among the family of a nation.
(iv) That our young men and young women may have friendship and cooperation with their counterparts in other parts of the world.
(v) That we may work for the development of our country.
(vi) That dominations and oppressions of minority nations in South-East Asia may be erased.
(vii) That the rule of Democracy may prevail in South-East Asia and peace and happiness be maintained.

6

Problem of Peace-Making in Mizoram

As I sat a lonely spectator of my country Mizoram is in full view before me. I was in a mood more of sentiment than of politics. The skies are very clear except a scattered clouds of silvery white here and there. The winter days are setting in and they are the most pleasant times of the year. The valley looks lovelier with its green tropical forests. The mountains and hills are blue, above which the silvery white clouds overhang, thus forming a match-making of the beauties. The horizons look very far and nothing is to be seen in the skies, except those Indian Air Force planes which carry out 'Secret Missions'. The land looks quiet and peaceful on the surface and no other outside world knows what is really going inside. None can tell of India is really doing against humanity by suppressing the rights of Mizo people with a host of murderers in the form of Indian Army who roam over the land and kill indiscriminately. That is her "Secret Mission" under the cloak of democracy and secularism. No outside world can see the treacherous killing of men, women and children in front of their petrified beloved ones. "I have given my life for my country", the crying of a dying freedom-fighter is still ringing unheard and unseen of them.

If one is asked for the reason of all this it may easily be said that India is doing her secret and unholy mission in Mizoram by bluntly ignoring the rights of Mizo people for their freedomhood and is militarily suppressing national aspiration. In other words, the denial of freedom to the Mizo people by India results in a great expense of human lives. What is then freedom? Freedom is the living law of principles of humanity like the law of gravity. It is, moreover, man's inherent sentiment to be his self in order to safeguard his personal respect. Any attempt by others to undermine this sentiment results in violence. This is natural. It exists under any circumstances. The standard and success of civilization is to be counted on how much far individual freedom and honour is respected in our society. Whenever there is suppression of one's freedom results in a reactionary violence. It is the work of human law to provide a just solution so that man as individual may live together in harmony on the basis of mutual respect. So also is the case of nations as individual persons. Greatness of a nation and success of its government are to be determined by what measure each individual enjoy his freedom of conscience and by what measure the principles of human rights prevail.

We have higher law called the international laws whose purpose is for the harmonious living of different national Groups on basis of mutual respect and upholding the 'Fundamental Human Rights'. By virtue of this law many oppressed nations had been liberated. The old imperialism have gone but a new colonialism is taking place under cover of democracy. So good as it is, it cannot be used effectively as it should be until now.

Freedom is synonymous with the principle of the Fundamental Human Rights. Wherever there is suppression of this right, there is no freedom. Notwithstanding the fact that the Indian Government with its unmatched superior powers is suppressing the rights of the Mizo people which it hoped to finish it in camera, disregarding the International sets of principles and morals. The Government of India and its papers say, "This is tribal uprising they are tribals who rebel against law and order" without giving reasons. Taking the same saying as a pretext to the outside world, India has been doing incessantly on her secret missions.

If the Mizo people, with their much higher literacy percentage to Indians are tribals, why Indians, who call themselves civilized, are not acting in a more civilized manner? In the manner they are carrying on with the atrocities the Indians are more of tribals. The Mizo people as a civilized nations wants to decide their political setup according to the International principle and the right of self-determination for nations. It is the Indian tribal attitude that stands on the way of sensible approach to this question of national rights.

On the question of the rights of nations for self-determination there have been much improvements in the understanding of the problem after World War II. Many oppressed nations were liberated accordingly and India herself is one of them. Many tribals have become great nations and there is no bar on the successive stages of their being called 'Tribals'. Yesterday they were tribals; today they are great nations. The term "tribal" is imperialist's coined word that has no logical consistency to the progress of mankind. It is the imperialist's pretext for the purpose of expansion and domination over minority nations.

I think Third World War is ever to come, come it may, there will again be more improvements of the understanding on the question on the rights of minority nations. Whatever form it may take, be it atomic or nuclear, the oppressed people, either tribal or non-tribal will be liberated. And this understanding of the question can no longer be hindered. The world after this Third War, I would call "the New World", in which I hope there will be more realistic approach to human rights problem; domination will be the logical victim of justice to be established there.

We, the oppressed people look forward to this Fourth World where surviving nations will be more brotherly with equal shares between the haves and the have-nots. The weak in the World will then become stronger, the strength of the present World will be swallowed up by their own might. Therefore, shall we not cease to struggle on unless India comes to understand and accept the Mizo people for their rights of self-determination sooner?

To implement its secret mission, the Indian Government kills us, burnt our houses and properties. They put thousands into prison. All this is unknown to the world outside, Indian atrocities and how it fabricates truth has all its purpose in the secret mission. For honest and realistic men of India, it may be surprising to know how their Government rulers have been manoeuvring things out.

They may not accept what has been done against Humanity by their rulers. For the same cause of national liberation the patriots of India had sacrificed themselves upon the altar of Indian Nationalism. This present act of the Indian Government to the people of Mizoram and Nagaland is against the principles she had fought twenty years ago. This betrayed the honest Indians who voted for them it has no conformity with the spirit of the Founders of India.

One may correctly assume Mizoram as a bundle of human sufferings unknown to others and without recognition. As such the Indian political manoeuvre paints the face of Mizoram in any manner they like, even up to giving themselves justice for murdering innocent people. Although there are various and numerous cases of the Indian Government atrocities and nefarious deeds which will take full volume, I would give only few incidents for instance, so that one may have an idea of how the secret mission is carried out.

On 13-2-1967 evening, the Indian troops harassed a church meeting of the Baptish Kohhran Hinschhe Paid (BKHP) Baptist Church Women Endeavour Group in Vuakmual village. The run-away women were shot like wild buffalo hunting in the prairies. One Secretary of the organization and other one girl were dead on the spot; many others were wounded. The Indians stayed the night encamping themselves in the Church and celebrated their victory as is often done in the Army canteen. Bullet holes on the Church walls are still to be seen.

On 9.6.1967, the Indian troops rounded up the people of Hnahchang village, and put them together in an open field. Commander of the troop (One Maj. Bakshi) opened fire at the mob. Eight people including women and children were dead on the spot; many were wounded. Their houses were used as funeral pyre as the Hindu practice, whereas the Mizo are Christians. Many wounded were not survived. They plundered the Church fund of Rs. 40. It was not wonder as they did wherever they go.

All India Radio on the subsequent nights broadcasted these incidents as if encounter between the Mizo rebel troop and the Indian Police Force; in which they claimed to have killed those dead. I do not think the Indians have forgotten the military term of encounter, but they have to forget it because they are carrying out secret missions. When, in March 1966, the whole business centre of Aizawl was burnt down by the Indian troops. The Indian Government said, "The Mizo Volunteers burnt it. When Aizawl, Tlabung, Marpara, Sangau, Hnahlan, Khawzawl and a number of civilian places were bombed resulting in the deaths and wounded of the civilians, including women and children at Mualcheng village, the Indian Government denied the action and said that its air force dropped supplies. They built Concentration Camps for which they said "Grouping Centre", while the inmates of the camps were sorrowfully crying, they said, "They are happy". This is how things were going under the secret mission. While they were burning the foodgrains of the villagers they starve the people of the Concentration camps. This is their design.

There were numerous torturous killings in violation of the Declaration of Human Rights. Many civilians were clubbed to dead on ground of suspicion. A number of village council presidents were torturously killed. In short, the Indian Military acts of atrocities to the people of Mizoram, I think, is a kind of most brutal suppression of human rights ever seen in this twentieth century. Almost all the Mizo Army personnel captured by Indian force were toturously killed; evem helpless wounded who came to be their prey fall on the same fate. Over and above, the Indian troops were excessive and enjoyed in shooting unarmed personnel. These acts are clear violation of Geneva agreements for principle of human treatment and treatment for prisoners of war to which India committed.

We, on our part, shall not change our political outlook in spite of the Indian atrocities rather as we committed to our own moral law in the light of the Geneva principles. We shall not cease to use our conscience and better judgement as we had demonstrated upon the many Indian military and civil persons who were under the hand of Mizo National Volunteers in 1966. I think they may testify justice and fair deal they had received under the Mizo Army and Police Authority. Ours is to uphold dignity of man; this we shall hold on to our friends and foes alike.

Years preceding to 1966, some section of the Mizo people had a notion that the Indian could perhaps become good friends and co-enterpriser in politics. Now their conception proved in a different way; they imbibe more with a doctrine of national imperative which grow in strength and stability day-by-day in spite of the cruel Indian suppression. I now, think that the Mizo people will be perverse to the last for their freedom.

To the Indians, being a Mizo is a crime punishable to death. This is how the Government of India is carrying on to fulfil its secret missions regardless of the International set of principles and morality. The United Nations Organisation, the one time Hope of the World for peace has been paralysed to fulfil its objectives. The so-called Human Rights Commission, which objectives are to uphold human rights and the principles of self-determination is now a dead horse. Our case is remarked "The Internal Matter of India" which bears no validity before the judgement of reason and it is just like passing judgement on an absentee's case. It has no logical consistency with the principles of humanity. The question of Internal or External should be decided by the people themselves in conformity with the rights of nations for self-determination.

Personally I am thinking over the capture of my wife and three children, all of them below five years of age, all are put into prison. What pleasure the Government of India has out of this? Has it anything to do with its secret missions? Perhaps it has! I could not find any legal consistency, either logic or consonance with ordinary practice of laws. If I were accused of a crime, should my family be also accused for no other reason, but only for being my wife and children? As far as memory could travel back there was time in the primitive stage of man that a man accused of crime was punished with all his close relations. But, in this twentieth century, even small children are difficult to convince that there was a time such system was practiced. The practice is tribal and outdated.

Almost all the families of the leaders of the Mizo people are now in prison. Those are: Pu Lalnunmawia (Vice President)'s wife and only son, Pu Sainghaka (Home Minister)'s wife and only baby son, Pu Lalkhawliana (Finance Minister)'s wife and children, Ngurkunga (Information & Broadcasting Minister) 's wife and children and many families of the high officials of the Government of Mizoram; so also thousands of others. Many children see the world through the prison bars for the first time. Many more learn to walk with the support of the prison walls. Do they commit any wrong? I don't think they do. But their parents, brothers and sisters resist against the Indian domination. Ah! That is their fault. Any sane person of the free world, how would you say to your children behind the iron bar?

Since the Indian politics takes the help of its army, then logic, truth, human value, justice—all are casualties. Indian political scheming pays little head to human value before her vast army who are roaming over the land; human life is cheap. A man is expandable for a slight mistake. What does a small nation matter? This hill tribal people occupy a very important strategic area for Indian defence, which liquidated them. This strategic area is more valuable for the defence of India in the event of Communist China aggression. Mizo people are a small price to pay for the defence of India. Let them die, they are expendable. After all the defence of India is more valuable. This is how the Indian Government rulers take the matter.

In the field of politics concerning the people of Mongoloid origin on the border of North-East India, the

Indian leaders cannot be concerned about truth. They are more of self-centred. They have no regard in the politics of the Mizo people and its consistence with truth. They are thinking to suppress the truth by organising propaganda of lie to bring change to Mizo leaders before their own people. All India Radio, mouthpiece of Lie, is broadcasting everything of political intrigue from the religious truth, humanities down to outright propaganda of lies. It is unholy as a harlot's cabin decorated with scripts of biblical passage. Preaching of religious sermons and propaganda of lies go freely hand in hand. They think to confirm political fabrication with biblical truth. They invited and organized self-seeking fanatics; nursed them with hatred; used them for their tools; and were given lump sum money for their price. They made them shout, "Away with freedom, we have no other king but India, who is kind enough to send army to our help and so did well to kill and imprisoned thousands of Freedom Fighters". These fanatics previously shouted, "Our religious Freedom is in danger. My country, wake up", It was that very India whom they feared. Their fear was that India would destroy their culture and people's solidarity. How imperfect man is!

This is how India was doing against human rights in Mizoram for her secret mission. Because these people are deprived of justice from the World Organisation, the Indian Government rulers are out with free hands to do whatever they please in the guise of Indian national integration even up to exterminating them. During their rule of almost two decades, they have been adopting a system of assimilation of the minority people. And now, they have been acting just like they have the ancient kings' pleasure of torturing other people for their fun. This is tribal, but they do not mind so long as it serves the purpose of their secret mission.

In our politics, we mean all is ordered with consistency to truth and humane principle. We place the infinite value of man and his freedom of conscience above everything. Our politics is a question of recognizing the principles of humanity. This is what India thinks that they know to suppress by using military force. But Indian leaders do not know that truth cannot ultimately be suppressed: that the sacrifices of the Mizo people upon the altar of national freedom is truth; that they demonstrate their national imperative; and this truth must prevail.

The question of the intrinsic value of human being with its political problem, and the Indian miscalculation of the question have now created Mizoram an arena of political fight. The fight is between contradictory views of the Indian giant and an active Mizo boy. The fight is unbalanced in all context. The boy fights because he has weapon of truth while the giant fights because he has superior might and power. This is a great contradiction on the plane of political problem on the question of the rights of man. Unless power sees reason the fight will go on till the giant frustrates. Sometimes truth is helpless before might. But truth never gives up hopes that the ultimate victory belongs to him. For the boy, the best means to win the Giant is, to teach him reasons. India needs reasons before anything else. Then only the solution on the rights of Mizo people will be possible.

Observing all possible avenues to this problem of national issue and its political impact, one thing I find that hinders justice and the work of peace is lack of understanding between the parties concerned. In the political issue of this kind, people of distinct nature always form a wrong opinion of others. This misguides them and as such become victims of their own miscalculations. Man who forms wrong opinion of his friend becomes victim of his own reaction to it. So also is India.

The Government of India, in its Constitution, labelled the distinct group of the people living in the highland region of the North East India as 'The Hill Tribal of Assam', even, after the chosen experimental ten-year-integration with the Indian Union in 1947 was ended in 1961. This is the wrong term imposed upon the people who call themselves 'MIZO' from their forefathers down to this generation. The people in this highland region are not tribals; the Mizo people are not tribals.

The Mizo people has their own national polity before the coming of British in 1871. They had their own Government similar to the Greek City States. After successive expeditions, the British Government brought Mizoram under its colonial occupation by annexing to the British India Empire in 1889. During the British occupation of almost sixty years, Mizoram had no connection with the British India or the Indian States. The affairs relating to the administration and that of external relation were under special responsibility of the Governor-General in Council as the Crown Representative. The Mizo people (who were then called 'Lushai') did not send any representative to the Indian Parliament or to the Provincial Assemblies. The status was same as Bhutan, that her internal matter was solely left to the Bhutanese people and in regard to her external relations, Governor-General in Council was responsible. We had no political relation with the British India or the Indian States.

During Japanese invasion in Second World War the Lushai Chiefs jointly issued a Manifesto to put up a stout resistance side by side with the Allied Powers. This has clarified the event that Mizoram had enjoyed full autonomy in her internal administration. Commenting on the joint declaration made by the Chiefs, Mr. M.C. McCall, the then Superintendent of Lushai Hills (now Mizoram) affirmed that it has been nothing short of the declaration made by England, Wales and Scotland to that effect. And he further reiterated that no country, shall claim the land after the war is over against the will of the people, since she was under responsibility of the allied power per order of the Atlantic Charter.

Following the declaration made by their chiefs many young Mizos joined in the army and formed a famed Lushai Brigade and Lushai Scouts. These brave men fought at Burma from till Japanese repulsion. The Mizo people also helped the Crown by sending more than two thousand contingents in Europe during First World War, and subsequently help was given in Abhor expeditions and in suppressing Haukip rebellion. All these helps given to the Crown by the Mizo people in time of war indicated a good relationship between the two. Accordingly Mizoram was granted autonomy by the British similar to certain autonomous power enjoyed by Bhutan under her colonial rule.

The Mizo people choose temporary integration with the free Indian Union in 1947 consequent on the transfer of power by the British with a condition that the Lushais (now Mizo) will be allowed to opt out of the Indian Union when they wish to do so, subject to a minimum period of ten years. In this the Mizo people reserve the right of self-determination. This is a clear point that they have no connection with Assamese or Indians except on their will. There is no reason for their being called tribals. The fact is that they are distinct national group and are quite different in outlook from that of Indians. The average intellectual potentialities and of the literacy are much higher than those of Indian average. They have their own cultural nobilities and character, national heroes and heroines. They have their outlook of life as the Indians have their own. There is no reason or justification for the attribution of this wrong nomenclature to the Mizo people. This is the Indian designs to fulfil her imperialist desire. This is the wrong opinion and misunderstanding of the Mizo people in particular and other highlanders by the Indians. This is the beginning of the present problem.

Having a quick restrospect to the temporary acceptance of joining the Indian Union in 1947, the Mizo Union, the first political party in Mizoram had stated to His Majesty's Government, the British Government; to the Government of British India and to its Constituent Assemblies for recognition of the Mizo people as a distinct national group; thereby giving any agreement to be reached with the Government of India are "subject to revision according to the future trend of events up to the extent of seceding after ten years. Fifty accredited leaders from political parties, churches, social workers and businessmen, held a meeting at Aizawl on 14th August, 1947 again stated to his Majesty's Government, the British Government, the Government of the British India and its Constituent Assemblies saying 'IF' and giving minimum ten years for the term of temporary integration after which it will be up to the people to decide.

The Government of India's response to these memoranda of the Mizo people is one of the saddest part in the political history of Mizoram. Mr. Jawaharlal Nehru, the late Prime Minister of India admitted that the Mizo people are not Indians and their country is not part of India. He further expressed his wish that relation be maintained for the interests of both countries. Shri B.N. Rao, the then Constitutional adviser of India, while he visited Aizawl, addressed a public meeting and said that the Mizo people had freedom of choice for either India or Burma or Pakistan or for their own independence. Moreover, he stated that Mizoram (then excluded area) is not part and parcel of India. The Indian Independence Act of 1947 has had no provision for the Mizo people except on their will.

Notwithstanding the fact that the Government of India was not honouring the memoranda of the Mizo people. Taking advantage of the political immaturity and playing the part of "false prophet" before the people, the Indian leaders did not make any reasonable response in regard to the context of the memoranda. Rather, their political intrigue put the Mizo people into an embarrassed situation. But the Mizo people would not give up their national stand under any circumstances. The question still awaits to be answered in accordance with the wishes of the people.

The Sixth Schedule of the Constitution of India (a part of the Constitution but not the Constitution itself) is solely laws for the administrative set-up of Mizoram and other hill regions. These provisons are temporary and are only for a term of ten years. The abolition of the Lushai chieftainship in Mizoram was compensated on the basis of ten years calculations. I do not say that this is the outcome of the memoranda of the Mizo Union and 50 accredited leaders. But on the other hand, I cannot believe this was done accidentally by the framers of the Indian Constitution. From the very beginning the affairs affecting the vital politics of the Mizo people was done behind the curtain unknown by the people concerned. One can only have guess work about this. This is the Indian political intrigue.

In the year 1956, when Mr. Nehru, the Late Prime Minister of India had a meeting with Mr. Phizo, President of the Naga National Council. Mr. Nehru requested him for temporary integration with the Indian Union for a term of ten years; after which it will be the will of the Naga people to decide for their future political set-up. Mr. Phizo refused the offer. Why India offered ten years. What is she trying to get out of it? If the offer was genuine and honest, and from the viewpoint of ordinary contract laws, I could hardly say that such agreement, had it been ever entered into, was out of order. But, now, I think Mr. Phizo had had reason to refuse and disbelieve the Indian intention. But, no matter whether Naga people accept India or not, the Indian

Government sends troops to Nagaland and suppress the people that now costs hundreds of lives.

Living together with the Indians, for almost twenty years the Mizo people by their own experience, now wants to reset their political set-up in the light of the memoranda of 1947. The Mizo people, thus, in their memorandum of 1965 demands the Government of India for a revision of their relations with Mizoram in respect of their right to self-determination. The leaders of the Mizo National Front, the largest political party in Mizoram, for a number of times put forward to the Government of India in writing and in verbal their keen desire for a round-table-talk with the Indian leaders to discuss the matter and find solution in peaceful means. To these, India paid no heed. Mizo leaders plainly stated to the Indian leaders that it is better to fight on a table than to fight in a battle field. In spite of this plea, India sent in her Army contingent, and the question of peaceful solution vanished in the air.

The demand of the Mizo people for recognition of their national status and for further recognition of their right of self-determination is a reasonable offer for peace with Indians with whom we have relation with the consent of the people. Any change in the political outlook of the people should be decided by the free will of the people; of course, with the concurrent goodwill of the Government of India on the basis of principles of the rights of nation. We want to make democratic decision in the dispute with India without interference of arms. But it is the Indian evasive attitude to the question that makes the whole affairs a mess.

The Government of India's reaction to the question of

the right of the Mizo people for self-determination is completely a miss. Not only they avoid to encounter the challenge of truth, but they adopted more treacherous political appeasement policy in the guise of special Development Scheme of Mizoram. This is the whitewash and behind it the real hand plays. Allured by their own miscalculation of the people's sentiment and forcing their way of systematic suppression as they have been doing so in Nagaland, the Indian Government sent in troops in the guise of road protection force. The treachery of their planned programme had been the cause of untold misery.

Under the clock of the Scheme large number of Indian service personnel and workers are infiltrated into Mizoram (Upto that moment no Indian is allowed to enter the land without documental permission). This is a system design for the cultural invasion against the social living of the Mizo people by the Indians whose motive is the assimilation of the minority nationals into Hindu way of living. For this and other of its kind the Central Government of India spends large sums of money and even buys influential persons among the minority nationals.

In the development scheme the real economic improvements of the people's living condition is totally nil. There is no production scheme of the land's resources. Moreover, all the markets which we used to enjoy during the British rule for vegetational products are closed under the Indian Government rule; the only business is purchase and sale of the Indian products among our own people which are in the hands of a few Marwaris (A rich Hindu class) playing from behind.

The question of economic development of Mizoram was one of the topmost topics among the people, during the years preceding 1966. Mizo leaders had many a time, put forward to the Government of India the need for the economic and social development of the land. Mizo District Council had made its utmost effort for the development works in spite of the fact that it could do nothing without the concurrent effort from the Indian Government. In fact, India had done nothing for the development of Mizoram worth mentioning.

The Mizo people are very keen in the development of their country. Their cooperation to the Government of India was second to none. They had constructed a Jeepable road from Aizawl to Lungleh of 128 miles long by their voluntary service in 1950-56. The road runs through the most difficult hills and mountainous terrains. By this, they demonstrated the craving heart for the development of their country. However, India was not interested to help those who can help themselves.

Therefore, it is evident that economic and social instability play equal important role in the then national aspiration of the people for sovereignty. The social and political outlook becomes more and more imbalance with the economic means and condition of the country. The people have realized the Indian Economic strangulation. Observing various aspects of the scheme of the Special Development of Mizoram, the main objective is the military purpose and other fields have only the names. It is now clear that when India says that the plan is completed, the resultant outcome for the Mizo people will surely be switching over to the more poverty and total suppression. Very this fact, I may recall the very word of Late Mr. Nehru. "Owing ...... their importance to India is its defence strategy....has the same bearing on the Indian Government policy matter concerning Mizoram. No matter, whatever the condition of the people may be, so long as the region serves the defence strategy to India, it is well and good."

The Mizo District Council, the puppet regime of the Government of India, is only a tool for moral degeneration. It functions as a colonial agent with its subsidiary corruptions. It is a puppet show to be denied and despised by the very people who made it for it cannot do anything to the people. It is an evil in the name of democracy. This has made politics in Mizoram an off-hand man job. It is made in the name of Mizo people but without effective authority. This is a mockery to the good name of democracy. The District Council was sometimes crippled by the Indian Government as a disciplinary action. The people, therefore, could not feel peaceful and become mentally unrest under this Indian intrigue and its Development Scheme.

The Mizo people have reason to disbelieve Indians because they have seen the lot of the other minority nationals who are now unknown except by their poverty and their being a fun-making group among the Indian public. Wherever they go, they are only cheating ponds which attract the Indian small businessmen and wayfarers.

The Mizo people have no other alternative but to uphold their rights to safeguard themselves and their interests, to ensure that their children may not be a fun-making group among the Indian public; and to do things for themselves with an obligation to respect the International laws and principles; and to be a good neighbour of other countries and especially of India. By then, the people hope that India will realize her responsibility to a small underdeveloped country, Mizoram on her border. However, India cannot see the point and is yet unable to understand the good intention of the Mizo people.

Mizo people loves, above everything, square meal and fair play, in all respects. It is their inborn sentiment inculcated in the spirit of '*Tlawmngaihna*' (Altruism) with its chivalry, hero and heroine. People want to develop their country and want to lift up their status to the level of other people. This is evident from the fact that when they hoped the real unity in diversity in India and tried to make it a success but enthusiastically co-operating India in all fields of public affairs. Younger generations have their own international outlook and desire to make friendships and contacts with their counterparts in other parts of the World. Contrary to this, India calls them "Tribal" who should not have such outlook. The due place for a tribal is the Indian Republic day's "Show-Case" in New Delhi where he can bloom with tribal decorations. Various tribals can be distinguished from their name-plates. Foreign Dignitaries enjoyed the fun, and India was proud to able to exhibit such variety of human specimen. India was happy to keep such variety of tribals for museum specimen; in fact, she had a lot. It was better for India to have such 'Republic Fun' with variety of tribals rather than developing them.

India, now, is dreaming to assuage the Mizo people for better social and economic development which has been craved for a long time ago. Her armies are constructing roads; they tell the people that because India loves Mizo people they make the roads. But the real purpose is to provide the Indian Army with operational facilities. Had India really been keen in the development of Mizoram, she should have done this half cost, she should have given Mizo people their proper share while the situation was all right. This is a mere pretext.

The Mizo people themselves feel most the need for the development of their country. In respect to their demand for national sovereignty, foreign observers might have been too much preoccupied in the absence of economic development in Mizoram. But it will be like putting the cart before the horse. Without political solution, there can be no economic development. In this turbulent period of Mizoram, the Indian Economic and 'Social White-washing', will serve no purpose. What development should a man have while his house, properties and grain-stores are burnt by their own troops. First of all, the political questions must be solved and then, the economic and social development will be added unto the Mizo people. This is the voice of truth; if India desires peace and development let her come forward without any motive. Let us be simple to reason together about truth.

Understanding of truth is always a difficult subject. While the progress in the understanding of science and technology is remarkably fast, the progress in the field of man-to-man understanding is comparatively slow, and the gap is still wide-open. If this gap is not narrowed down man will be victims of his own inventions. The so-called major powers and the so-called civilized people will be the more sufferers, if not totally eliminated. This causes anxiety all over the world and there can be no substantial improvement in the man-to-man understanding. Someday it may totally fail; then the Third World War; then the Fourth World War.

Up to the present days understanding between the Mizo people and the Indian Government rulers have been in a hopeless state. The Government of India, undermining all the human principles and morality believes in the might of its arms to be able to suppress the political aspiration of the Mizo people, and to completely root out all the elements which are considered anti-State activities. To this, Mizo people are reacting violently. All India Radio, the trumpet of propaganda, repeatedly announces that the Mizo nationalists (she calls rebels) are only few people and they are now nearly vanquished. Meanwhile, my jungle city 'LIBARTY' grows instability day-by-day. Mizo people are fighting for their freedom is not kind to be vanished, military victory or defeat has no meaning for the freedom fighters. Freedom fighting is the highest quality of spirit which prevails under any circumstances. The spirit does not count strength in military term. It does not mind defeat, it will go on from generation to generation; its abode is in the deep hearts of the people. Guns or without gun, it shall never leave its abode. It is a first-class mistake that India does not like to see the truth. She, moreover, believed that the problem could be solved in the battle-field; then, throttle the very truth, the rights of the Mizo people for self-determination in secrecy and with a political silencer.

The people, rather than submitting to the Indian military threat of extermination, take more resolute and determined resistance against such menace. They have found themselves now in what their leaders had said years back. They find their fight is worth fighting. They grow in strength and stability day-by-day. It is evident from a simple villager of Hmuntlang who was watching the burning fire of his house with all his properties by Indian troops and says, "You may burn my house, you may also burn my properties, but you shall never burn my heart". It was also a sarcastic statement from a captured boy of fourteen years old, who was going to be shot by the Indian soldiers near Sangau village. He was given his last time and was asked to make note on the incident to his parents, which he says, "....One hour from now, I am going to be shot by those (Indians) who are serving for my country." "Be not grieve nor weep, I have done my duty," he went on. The spirit of the Freedom fighters shall never die; the spirit and blood of the martyrs shall be calling upon the future generations. Freedom of the Mizo people is imperative; it is a rising Sun, no one will ever subdue it by arms.

Whenever India finds vulnerability in the political problems of this kind by military means, she does not hesitate to substitute might for Justice. We have seen this case in Hyderabad, Kashmir, Goa, Nagaland and now in Mizoram. Except in Hyderabad and Goa, India fails in all her attempts. Arms is seldom a successful weapon for peace.

The case of the Mizo people is not a military question.

It is neither chauvinist dogma nor doctrinal fanaticism, nor tribal fantasy. It is a question of recognition to humanity. It is a political question and the solution lies in a political settlement. The solution lies in the acceptance of the principle of co-existence. Mizo people wants to live side by side with the Indian people. They want to live in peace and good neighbourliness with India, Pakistan, Burma and all other countries. They do not want to be tribals of none of the neighbouring people. They want to develop their country with the help of India and other neighbouring countries and lift up their social and economic status to the level of their neighbouring people. Most of all they want peace and happiness with Indians and all the people all over the world. Therefore, the Indian military adventured in a vain enterprise. If India can realize this before long, I think both of us will be beneficiaries.

The physical defence strategy of Mizoram is a good thing for India. India, thus wants to retain Mizoram for ever for a battle field in case of external attack from Communist China or Burma or Pakistan. But Physical defence strategy is not all important for defence of a country in this age of ideological war. The more important strategy for defence of a country lies in the hearts of the people. India is fortunate enough to have a first class natural defence in the Himalayan mountain barriers in case of attack from the North Communist countries. But it is likely that the communist would attack India by that way. While the Indian armies take position in the Himalayans to repulse the Communist China attack, the heart of India is not safe from Communism. Communist China may attack

India in Kerala, Bengal, Assam and even in the Hindi-protagonist States of Northern India. In the like manner, India may have guns battle with China in Mizoram, still the hearts of the Indian people would fall into Communism. Himalayans are not all important for India's defence; again, Mizoram is not by far, important for the defence of India unless she can have the hearts of the Mizo people.

The Indian Government has had a firm politics in the Himalayan Kingdoms such as Sikkim, Bhutan and other areas in the North East Frontier Agency (Now Arunachal Pradesh). Because of their important positions in the defence strategy to India. It is well and good so long as she wins the heart of these people and there is no question as to its compatibility with the natural laws or with the International morality.

Now the question of the Nagaland comes into the picture. It is all the same that India thinks Nagaland is essential for the Defence Strategy to India and she tries to hold on it with whatever expense in money and blood; that is the reason why India still occupies Nagaland in spite of utmost resistance by the Naga people. Nagaland, now becomes the vulnerable points of Indian defence. Why then? Because India cannot have the hearts of the people. The Naga people now seeks friendship with comrades in Peking. We cannot blame them, and there is nothing wrong of them in seeking relation with the comrades in parts of the world. Ideology or no ideology, they have to have friends who could sympathise them and help them in their protracted struggle for freedom. Naga people needs many things, many things more to achieve their political objectives. They cannot be concerned about the morality of one who gives them aid; nor consider the morality of giving aid. Aid is that matters most. For this, the Naga people are not desperado. Their objective is genuine as much as India has her objectives for the Indian people. But the saddest point is that, under the Indian military repression, a Naga youngmen can only be happiest to see a gun in his arms. Still would India consider Nagaland's importance to the defence strategy of India.

The Government of India claims Mizoram as the integral part of India and the dispute as in her internal matter. This view is one-sided and the validity of the term should not be considered *ex parte* view and version, of course, this view has some legal sense, but void of principles. It also has its limitation up to a certain condition. The Indian Government has that consideration sole within the framework of the Constitution. However, the dispute in the case of the Mizo people is not a constitutional problem, a legal remedy should not have far, because the Indian Constitution is a composition of good laws.

The dispute, rather, is concerned with the principles of humanity. Ordinary laws are apt to be amended whenever they are found incompatible with certain sets of principles. It is, thus, principles and beliefs based on the equitability of rights that makes law; not the laws that make principles and belief. It will, therefore, be totally amiss if the dispute on the question of the Rights of the Mizo people *vis-à-vis* the Indian Government's stand and version is taken in the view point of its Constitution alone. The Mizo people never protest against the articles of the Constitution of India and they would never question about the Constitution of India. Therefore, the solution of the dispute in the case of the Rights of the Mizo people does not lie in the Constitutional amendments of rescinding some part of it. The solution lies only in the acceptance of the "Universal Declaration of Fundamental Human Rights", and consequently, to give the Mizo people their due place in it and to let them decide for their own. The so-called India's police action and her belief in killing more will serve no purpose but will only multiply hatred.

In the case of the Mizo people on their rights, the question of internal or external is not concerned with the Geopolitics of India. It is, rather, the sentiment of the people that concern about the question. Till 1947, the Mizo people had their own territorial integrity and this was respected by the British Government. When they choose temporary integration with India in 1947, it was one of the demands that India should respect the territorial integrity of Mizoram. It will, therefore, be wrong if India takes the question in the light of geopolitics.

In this question, it is the sentiment of the people that matters most. If democracy is to prevail, the question must be put to the conscience of the people. The basic principles of democratic decision is only with the people; free will and consent should prevail without interference of arms. If anything is done without the consent of the people will amount domination. If any other people can impose their rule over another people without the consent of that another people's consent, it is suppression of the will of that people. If anything is done undermining the sentiment of the Mizo people, it is wrong as the old colonial rule. It is imperialism because it undermines the democratic principles and civilized outlook of life. It is barbaric because it lacks decency and believes in the rule of the might. If the Government of India continues to impose conditions, or in a clear language, dominate us, this is against our will and consent. Unless she gives herself colonial licence in spite of her professed principles, she must stop this complication of international question. And, then, the question will be settled with a rule of democratic principles and the free will of the Mizo people must prevail.

During this short career of my political life, I have made a number of contacts with foreign diplomats and individuals, I have made them clear of my country's position and the people's stand. All of them agreed with the stand of the Mizo people and they seemed concerned about the political complications of the matter. In view of the armed repressive measures in Nagaland and its political entanglement that makes democratic hitch, they were pre-occupied with the multitude of the problem. They were not wrong. We have known that India is very big in the problem and there is no decency in her dealing with the matter. Any way, Mizoram needs peace at any cost.

Man's strife for peace is a constant battle. The largest World forum we have at the present days is the United Nations Organisation. The General Assembly of the United Nations is a battle-field for peace where diplomats fight with conscience and tact. But the problem is there that the battle cannot be finished in the Assembly premises alone. It has, now, become a complement to the gun powder in the battle field. The U.N. has many outstanding problems and pending cases and this is overburdening it. If another problem is added to it, this 'Old Horse' may collapse some day soon. What will then come next? The Fourth World! Don't worry friends. It is a destined World for man's happiness whether it is here or up there.

Now the U.S. is bombing Hanoi for peace; the North Vietnam and the Viet Cong (the National Front for Liberation) are furiously trying to push out America from the South Vietnam, for peace. All statements all over the world express concern and wish for peace in Vietnam. Most of the world's opinions are compatible on a proposition that the Vietnamese people are to determine for themselves without any foreign interference. The U.N. Secretary General U Thant while he visited countries in the South-East Asia in 1967, stated that the Vietnam war is a nationalist struggle and thus the solution lies only with the people themselves. He pressed the U.S.A. to stop bombing of North Vietnam to make ways for negotiation. Unto the present days America continues bombing of the North Vietnam and no one can interfere in her intention. It is a general apprehension that victory is not belonging to the U.S.A. U.S.A. may win the war in Vietnam but she shall never win the real war, the nationalist spirit. Hanoi may not win the war in the battle field, but it is likely that she may win in Washington. President Johnson expresses his concern about this. China, ruler of the other world cannot be overlooked in this affair and other hot spots of the world.

She will scratch any scrap of the world issues. In spite of American huge armament and dollars, China is trying hard for her programme of 'International Communism' for durable peace in the world. Neither China nor U.S.A. is the question in the Vietnam war. But it is the sentiment of the Vietnamese people and the Nationalists' spirit that shall win the war under any circumstances.

Mizoram do not believe in any foreign interference, nor seek any. What the Mizo people concern most is the good heart and understanding of the Indian Government. All things in the context of the Indian Government calculations are not a difficult subject of compromise if the basic stand of the Mizo people is recognized. In the defence strategy, we are here, who may need a good friend for Indian protection. The defence of India is the defence of Mizoram, her security is our security. If the giant brother nearby falls, a solitary boy cannot stand; if Mizoram falls the defence of India will be in jeopardy. More of that, peace is a best defence of a country.

Concerning the human rights, it has been the headache of this late twentieth century and this has been the basic cause of troubles all over the world—such as, Kashmir, Nagaland, Israel *vis-à-vis* Arabs, Rhodesia, South Vietnam, South-West Africa, the Black American Negroes and lately Mizoram. We have Human Rights Commissions and Decolonization Committee of the U.N. subordinate bodies. They are very far to hear the voices of oppressed slaves with whom they cannot, in fact, have interest. They cannot care how many slaves have been killed and are going to be killed today, or tomorrow, so long as they uphold the human rights, the slaves' masters' rights. They cannot care who are exterminating and who are exterminated, so long as the might survives whose rights are much more easy to be uphold. For these and other variety of imperfect nature of human being, I am thinking of my late father whose poverty I inherit and now, my beloved wife and children, who are waiting for me behind the prison bar of India. It is indeed, a poor slave ought to pay his wife and children for his freedom.

At the close of my statements on the question of the Rights of Mizo people for Self-Determination *vis-à-vis* the Government of India's stand and reaction with its aftermath bloody conflict, and in my private search for peace and for total abolition of arms, and for starting a new living side by side on basis of mutual respects, honouring dignity of human persons, for maintenance of justice in all sphere of life, and to live the life in conformity with the international order, the following propositions are in my mind.

Greater efforts must be given to convince the Government of India that our existence as a distinct national unit on the border of India and will not be a menace to India's security.

We must indefatigably try to impress the Government of India that having the chance to exercise our right to self-determination is the only ways and means for a peaceful and harmonious living side by side with the people of India. However, hard it may be on the part of the latter in order to achieve the best interests of both the parties.

On the other hand, India would accept the rightful existence of the Mizo people and respect as human persons.

She should accordingly recognize our rights of self-determination as stated in our memorandum of the 14th August, 1947, and further, give allowance to a democratic means of settling the dispute without interference of arms.

I wish the Government of India to amend all her misunderstandings about us bearing in mind a more realistic approach to the question of the rights of Mizo people, and also to show a bold effort for the settlement of the dispute on the basis of mutual respects in the light of international morality. On our part we are ready as ever for a just and honourable settlement. Let us work together for peace.

Appendix I

MEMORANDUM OF 50 ACCREDITED MIZO LEADERS (1947)

Proceeding of a meeting of the accredited leaders of the Lushai Political Parties held at Aizawl on 14th August, 1947

Chairman : (elected) Mr. L.L. Peters, Superintendent of Lushai Hills.

Present

1. Khawtinkhuma, M.A.
2. R. Thanhlira, B.A.
3. Vanthuama
4. Pastor Chhuahkhama
5. Brig. Kawlkhuma, S.A.
6. Khuma
7. Lalbuaia
8. Hrangaia
9. Muka
10. Rosiama
11. Vanchhunga
12. Chawnghnuaia
13. Phillipa
14. Capt. Ngurliana, S.A.

15. Pachhunga
16. Vanlawma
17. Vankhama
18. Laihnuna
19. Chhunruma
20. Pastor Zairema, B.Sc,. B.D.
21. Rina
22. Zawla
23. Sena
24. Rosema
25. Lalupa
26. Lalhnema
27. Pastor Saiaithanga
28. Pastor Liangkhaia
29. Lalbiakthanga, M.A.
30. Lairopuia
31. Suaka
32. Hmingliana
33. Lalana
34. Lianhnuna, B.A.
35. Pasena
36. Lalsailova Chief.
37. Lalbuanga Chief
38. Lalzuala Chief
39. Lamlira Chief
40. Kamlova
41. Ch. Ngura Chief
42. Zami (Mrs. K.T. Khuma)
43. Kaptulhaii
44. Biakveli (Mrs. Buchhawna)

45. Lalrongenga, Ex. Subedar
46. Thanseia, Ex. Subedar
47. R. Zuala, Ex. Subedar
48. Dahrawka, V.A.S.
49. Kapthianga
50. Saphlira, B.A.

1. Resolved that owing to the unexpected acceleration of the date of transfer of powers by the British Government and as the Lushais have as yet been definitely informed in details as to what is to be the proposed future constitution and form of administration of the district and as Section 7 sub-section (1) of the Indian Independence Bill does not clarify the situation, it is accordingly thought necessary that His Excellency, the Governor of Assam should kindly inform them in writing as to what these are also to whether Lushais are at this stage allowed the option of joining any other dominion, i.e., Pakistan or Burma.

Resolved further that Superintendent of Lushai Hills should kindly communicate the above request of the Lushai to the Adviser to His Excellency, the Governor of Assam in order to clarify these points.

2. Resolved that if the Lushais are to enter into the Indian Union. Their main demands are:

(i) That the existing safeguard of their customary laws and land tenure, etc., should be maintained.

(ii) That the Chin Hills Regulations 1896 and Bengal Eastern Frontier Regulation 1873 should be retained until such time as the Lushais themselves through their District Council or other parallel district authority declare that these can be abrogated.

3. That the Lushai will be allowed to opt out of the Indian Union when they wish to do so, subject to a minimum period of ten years.

No. 6927-76
G. of 21.8.1947

Sd/.
L.L. Peters (14.8.47)
Superintendent,
Lushai Hills

Copy forwarded to all the leaders who took part in the proceedings.

Forwarded by:

Sd/.	Sd/.
Sainghinga	L.L. Peters (14.8.47)
Asstt. Superintendent	Superintendent,
	Lushai Hills

Appendix II

MEMORANDUM OF MIZO NATIONAL FRONT (1965)

Memorandum submitted to the Prime Minister of India by the Mizo National Front

General Headquarters: Aizawl, Mizoram on 30th October, 1965

This memorandum seeks to represent the case of the Mizo people for freedom and independence, for the right of territorial unity and solidarity for the realization of which a fervent appeal is submitted to the Government of India.

The Mizo from time immemorial lived in complete dependence without foreign interference. Chiefs of different class ruled over separate hills and valleys with supreme authority and their administration was very much like that of the Greek city-states of the past. Their territory or any part thereof had never been conquered or subjugated by their neighbouring states. However, there had been border disputes and frontier classes with the neighbouring people which ultimately brought the British Government to the scene in 1844. The Mizo country was subsequently brought under the British political control in December 1895, when a little more than half the country was arbitrarily carved out and named LUSHAI HILLS (now

Mizo District) and the rest of their land was parcelled out of their hands to the adjoining people for the sole purpose of administrative convenience without obtaining their will or consent. Scattered as they are divided, the Mizo people are inseparably united together by their strong bond of tradition, custom, culture, language, social life, and religion wherever they are. The Mizo stood a separate nation, even before the advent of the British Government having a nationality distinct and separate from that of India. In a nutshell, they are distinct nation, created, moulded and nurtured by God and Nature.

When the British India was given a Dominion status by promulgation of the Constitution Act of 1935, the British Government having fully realized the distinct and separate nationality of the Mizo people, decided that they should be excluded from the purview of the Constitution and they were accordingly classed as an EXCLUDED AREA in terms of the Government of India Order 1936. Their land was then kept under the special responsibility of the Governor-General in Council in his capacity as Crown Representative, and the Legislature of the British India had no influence whatsoever.

In other words, the Mizo had never been under the Government of India and never had any connection with the politics and policies of the various groups of Indian Union. When India was in the threshold of Independence the relation of the Mizo with the British Government and with the British India were fully realized by the Indian National Congress leaders. Their leader and spokesman Pandit Jawahar Lal Nehru released a press statement on

19th August, 1946 and stated, "The tribal areas are defined as being those along frontiers of India which are neither part of India, nor of Burma, nor of any Indian States, nor of any foreign power". He further stated, "The areas are subsidized and the Governor General's relation with the inhabitants are regulated by *sanads*, custom or usage. In the matter of internal administration the areas are largely left to themselves." Expressing the view of Indian National Congress he continued, "Although the tribal areas are technically under the Sovereignty of His Majesty's Government, their status, when a new constitution comes into force in India, will be different from that of Aden, over which the Governor General no longer has executive authority. Owing to their inaccessibility and their importance to India in its defence strategy their retention as British possession is more unlikely, one view is that with the end of sovereignty in India, the new Government of India (i.e., Independent Government of India) will enter into the same relation with the tribal areas as the Governor General maintains now unless the people of these areas choose to seek integration with India".

From the foregoing statement made by Pandit Jawahar Lal Nehru and the Constitution Act of 1935 it is quite clear that the British Government left the Mizo Nation free and independent with the rights to decide their future political destiny.

Due solely to their political immaturity, ignorance and lack of consciousness of their fate, representative of the Mizo Union, the largest political organization at that time, and fifty accredited Mizo leaders representing all political organizations including representatives of religious denomination and social organizations that were in existence, submitted their demand and choose integration with free India imposing conditions, *inter alia* "THAT THE LUSHAIS WILL BE ALLOWED TO OPT OUT OF INDIAN UNION WHEN THEY WISH TO DO SO, SUBJECT TO A MINIMUM PERIOD OF TEN YEARS".

The political immaturity and ignorance which led the Mizo people to the misguided choice of integration with India was the direct result of the ban by the British Government of any kind of political organization till April 1946 within Mizo land which was then declared 'apolitical area'.

During the fifty years of close contact association with India, the Mizo people have not been able to feel at home with Indians or in India, nor have they been able to feel that their joys and sorrows have really ever been shared by India. They do not, therefore, feel Indian. Being created separate nation they cannot go against the Nature to cross the barrier of nationality. They refused to occupy a place within India as they considered it to be unworthy of their national dignity and harmful to the interest of posterity. Nationalism and patriotism inspired by political consciousness has now reached its maturity and the cry for political self-determination is the only wish and aspiration of the people, *ne plus ultra*, the only final and perfect embodiment of social living for them. The only aspiration and political cry is the creation of Mizoram, a free and sovereign state to govern herself, to work out her own destiny and to formulate her own foreign policy.

To them Independence is not even a problem or subject of controversy, there cannot be a dispute over the subject nor could there be any difference of opinion in the matter. It is only a recognition of human rights and to let others live in the dignity of human persons.

While the present world is strongly committed to freedom and self-determination of all nations, large or small and to promote of fundamental human rights, and while the Indian leaders are strongly wedded to that principle, taking the initiative for and championing the cause of Afro-Asian countries, even before the world body, particularly deploring domination and colonization of the weaker nations by the stronger, old or new, and advocating peaceful co-existence, settlement of international dispute of any kind through the medium of non-violence and in condemning weapons that can destroy the world, and in general wishing of goodwill towards mankind. The Mizo people with their aspiration for freedom and independence, per principle that no one is good enough to govern another man without that man's consent.

Though known as headhunters and a martial race, the Mizo commit themselves to a policy of non-violence in their struggle and have no intention of employing any other means to achieve their political demands. If on the other hand the Government of India brings exploitative and suppressive measures into operations employing their military might against the Mizo people as is done in the case of the Nagas which God forbid, it would be equally erroneous and futile for both the parties for a soul cannot by destroyed by weapons.

For this end it is in goodwill and understanding that the Mizo nation voices her rightful and legitimate claim of full self-determination through this memorandum.

The Government of India in their turn and in conformity with the unchallenged global truth expressed resolved among the text of Human Rights by the United Nations in its august Assembly that in order to maintain peace and tranquillity among mankind, every nation, large or small may, of right, be free and independent shall set the Mizo Nation free to work her own destiny to formulate her own internal and external policies and shall accept and recognize her political independence. Would it not be a selfish active and design of India and would it not amount to an act of offence against humanity, if the Government of India claim Mizoram as a part of their territory and try to retain her as their possession against the national will of Mizo people simply because their land is important for Indian defence strategy?

Whether the Mizo Union should shed her tears in joy, to establish and form lasting friendship with India in war and in peace, or in sorrow and in anger, is up to the Government of India to decide.

S. Lianzuala	Laldenga
General Secretary	President
Mizo National Front	Mizo National Front
Mizoram	Mizoram

Dated Aizawl
The 30th October, 1965

Appendix III

FOREIGN MINISTER (MNF) CLARIFIED MIZO STAND

Zoram, June 1968

Pu Lalhmingthanga, Foreign Minister clarified stand of the Mizo people in respect of the present conflict with the Government of India. He said, "Mizo people are fighting for the principle of humanity which ultimately demands their political freedom. Our stand is in conformity with the Declaration of Human Rights and so far as our relation with India is concerned we cannot be less than human being. During the years preceding 1966 we had clearly stated, often times, in verbal and in writing to the Government of India our stand and sincere desires for peaceful solution and in a non-violent means. But it is the uncompromising attitude of the Government of India and its intention to dictate such solution within its own terms with support of its military might that hinders the work of peace. This has now resulted in a great expense of lives and properties.

"Mizo people, he continued, are as ever desirous of peaceful settlement of their problem with India and still pursue to that end. In the mean time they cannot do anything with the Government of India which falls short of human status. Indian thinks to suppress our rights by employing her military might and by organizing propaganda of lies; now, we are suffering exceedingly under the cruel hands of Indian army. Our menfolks are inhumanly killed without justice by the Indian troops. This is a clear indication of Indian lack of understanding of human values. Yet we are very firm in our stand which is truth and we will persevere under the amount of Indian atrocities for we know that truth cannot ultimately be suppressed. How many of us have suffered death and how much more India is willing to kill to realize the truth which is a question yet to be known. We will not, however, give up our search for peace in Mizoram and we would welcome any Indian move provided it is ordered with consistency to the basic principles of our rights.

Our need for peace is basic. We need peace to live as human being, to build our houses wherever we wish, not necessarily within Indian Concentration Camps; and to till our fields to earn our daily needs. But, instead, we are inhumanly tortured and killed, our people are harassed with guns and mortar bombs, our homes are burnt and we are driven like cattle into the Concentration Camps; our fields are uncared and are grown with weeds as a result of Indian Design of forced famine. The Geneva Agreement for Principle of human treatment is without effect for the Mizo people. In short, the Indian brutality is excessive.

However, our appeal to the conscience of Indian leaders is to no longer undermine the truth contained in the rightful stand of Mizo people for which safeguard we have been giving ourselves and go on giving with whatever amount it demands. The Indian military adventure is a vain enterprise which is simply degenerating a democratic conscience and decency of our civilization. There cannot be defeat or victory and the problem is not a military question. It is rather a question of recognizing the principles of humanity in relation to Mizo people. What we want is, therefore, peace in our land that guarantees freedom and nothing else. From this of our stand we cannot simply budge.

Note: This statement was published in *Dampa Weekly* on June 1968.

Appendix IV

PEACE-MAKING IN MIZORAM

Without doubt any peace loving man would want to have peace in this land. The Indian leaders want peace, or so they say. Our social, political and religious leaders want peace. In fact, all the Mizo people want peace and we pray our present conflict with India to stop.

The great misunderstanding between the Mizo people and rulers of the Government of India has fallen the lives of many people with the great loss of great wealth and properties on both sides. What a miserable misunderstanding ! The present conflict between the Government of India and the Mizo people is mainly politics in nature and a pity is that no political standing and rehabilitation is yet possible or the cause of this miserable conflict is not removed. To remove the cause of the trouble is no mere problem for it is necessary for both the conflicting parties to come to reason together and to arrive at a certain level of good understanding which may obviously come to the loss of some interests of each of the party. So is the problem of making peace.

Before and after 1966, India seems openly concerned only to get her political interest out of the political rights of the Mizo people. We can say this because the Indian leaders have let down the Mizo people by ignoring their appeal for a peaceful solution of the Mizo problem and by passing the memorandum of 1965 as not important. Up to the present day India seems amusing herself with the wild idea to suppress the rights of the Mizo people because the Government of India will not hear of any appeal from the Mizo leaders for peaceful negotiation for solution of the Mizo problem.

Violence is not corrective measure. Never in the history of mankind is there to find how and where violence has permanently solved any problem of mankind. In the course of three years' armed conflict between India and the Mizo people we can see that violence is feeding only its bitterness in the human hearts full to the brim of the cup of hatred and enmity. At any rate, any man can testify the wisdom of the truth that the end of might is but destruction for all.

It is a miserable misunderstanding to use violence on both the sides to achieve our political interests. It is miserable because violence is of destruction. The fact that it is a misunderstanding is the lame consideration of violence by both the parties as the only instrument for solution of differences.

The Mizo leaders want peace with India which is based upon human understanding in the light of the present conflict. Violence is bringing the horrors of many irreparable loss of human lives and properties; tortures our bodies and weakens our souls. The Mizo leaders shall do anything in their power to help save the people if it does not come to barter away the bodies and souls of the Mizo people. But it is India who is mainly responsible for all these sufferings of the present day. It is a blunder mistake on her part to seek an armed solution of the Mizo problem. Sooner the Indian leaders realized and take the stock of the futility to use violence against the Mizo people the better will be the chance to remove the cause of this miserable misunderstanding.

The Mizo people in general want peace with India which is coming only out of good understanding and love. We cannot be so anxious to see the end of the present conflict between India and the Mizo people had it not been stopped by love and understanding here and now. At any rate, there can be no peace between two conflicting parties unless there is a compromise and understanding through peaceful negotiation. We all had enough experience from the study of human history that if one conflicting party was too full of prejudice against the other that such an act of malevolence usually drove the other party to fight for his party to the last. In this present conflict so also we can see an endless retaliation and counter-retaliation if India is being the party to go on pursuing the policy of assimilation of minority party with whatever means they have.

And once again in this present conflict between India and the Mizo people, none of the other people is equally responsible as are the Indian leaders and the leaders of the Mizo National Front to bring to stop this conflict. From this same point of view it is not unimportant to bring to the sense of some people and that of the few local political groups in particular, not to minimize the consequence of any intervention in the dealing with the problem of making peace. It will be a failure and blundering, too. If any party cuts itself into the business with wild hope to accumulate some interest only for that party.

Peace-making is a noble vocation. To make peace it requires a man a great deal of courage and good understanding to humanity and also the knowledge of noble principles to guide the conscience. None, however, great the intensity of his desire might have been, can subscribe any valuable material to the making of peace in Mizoram if he does not come to full consciousness of how to make peace. It is a pity, therefore, that some of us do not seem to know what is this and what is that because we are mainly guided by a notion that 'ours is right' or that our idea of peace is to come only to the best interest of our party.

Appendix V

MNF DECLARATION OF INDEPENDENCE

In the course of human history it becomes invariably necessary for mankind to assume their social, economic and political status to which the Law of Nature and Nature's God entitles them. We hold this truth to be self-evident that all men are created equal, and that they are endowed with inalienable fundamental human rights and dignity of human person; and to secure these rights. Governments are instituted among men deriving their just power from the consent of the governed and whenever any form of Government becomes destructive of this end, it is the right of the people to alter, change, modify and abolish it and to institute a new government and laying its foundation on such principles and organizing its power in such forms as to them shall see most likely to affect their rights and dignity. The Mizo created and moulded into a nation and nurtured as such, by Nature's God have been intolerably dominated by the people of India in contravention of the Law of Nature.

The leaders of the Mizo Nation had, many a time, verbally and in writing, put forward to the Government of India, their desire of self-determination for creation of free and Independent Mizoram for bringing about protection of Human Rights and Dignity, which the Mizo, by nature, ought to have, but the Government of India, violating the Charter of the United Nations and its Universal Declaration of Human Rights reaffirmed in the principles of Bandung Conference, have ignored the voice of the Mizo people and are determined to continue domination and colonization ruling over us with tyranny and despotism by instituting self-designed administrative machinery with which they endeavour to mislead the world to win their confidence.

Our people are despised, persecuted, tortured, manhandled and murdered without displaying justice while they preach and profess before us and throughout the world that they have instituted for us a separate administrative set-up in conformity with the principles of Democracy. To conceal their evil and selfish design religious assimilation and Hindu indoctrination they preach to have established which we cannot accept as it leads to suppression of Christianity.

To prove this, let facts be submitted to the candid world:

1. They have instituted government to rule over us in our own country without any respects for Human Rights and Dignity even in the fact of the present candid world which is committed to these rights and dignity.
2. They have been pursuing a policy of exploitive measures in their attempt to wipe out Christianity, sole religion, and no consideration has ever been paid to our national way of life.
3. They have been preaching throughout the world as

if they have instituted a separate administrative machinery in conformity with the principles of Democracy to conceal their policy of generation of our national morality and of assimilation while what had been instituted for us is a pattern of colonial administration.

4. They refused not only to procure supply of food and arrange other forms of assistance in times of famine, but also prohibited us from seeking and receiving assistance from friendly countries, which resulted in the death of many people.
5. They have established a multitude of offices and sent hitherto swarms of Indian officers, who had an immoral life cruelly appeasing our womenfolk to commit immorality with them by taking advantage of their social capacity and of the position they occupy in the administrative machinery.
6. Taking the advantage of economic frustration of the people they subject us to economic slavery and force us to enter into the door of poverty.
7. Curbing freedom of expression, our patriots are arrested and kept in jails without displaying any form of justice.
8. The export facilities which we used to enjoy during the pre-Indian domination, has been totally closed.
9. Without exploring our country's economic resources in agriculture, industries and mining and giving no consideration for their development, they maintain suppressive measures against our economic right.

10. Realising the importance of our country to India in its defence strategy, the Government of India is establishing military basis throughout our country and thereby creating an atmosphere of cold war while nothing is done for its economic and social development.
11. In spite of our repeated appeal for peaceful settlement of our rightful and legitimate demand for full self-determination, the Government of India is bringing exploitive and suppressive measures employing their military might and waging war against us as done in the case of the Nagas and the Kashmiris.
12. Owing to absence of medical facilities in our countries, our people died without having medical treatment and attention.

For these and all other innumerable causes, we declared to the candid world that India is unworthy and unfit to rule over the civilized Mizo people who are created and moulded into a nation and nurtured as such and endowed with territorial integrity by Nature and Nature's God.

We, therefore, the Representatives of Mizo people, meeting on this day, the first of March, in the year of our Lord, nineteen sixty-six appealing to the Supreme Judge of the World for the rectitude of our intention. So, in the name and by the authority of the good people of this country solemnly publish and declare, that the Mizoram is, and of rights ought to be free and independent, that they are absolved from allegiance to India and its

Parliament and all Political connections between them and to Government of India is and ought to be dissolved and that as free and independent state, they have full power to levy war, conclude peace, contract alliances, establish commerce and to do all other acts and things which independent State may have right to do. And for the support of this Declaration, we mutually pledge to each other with a firm reliance on the Protection of Divine Providence, our lives, our fortunes, and our sacred Honour. We appeal to all freedom loving nations and individuals to uphold Human Rights and Dignity and to extend help to the Mizo people for realization of our rightful and legitimate demand for self-determination. We appeal also to all independent countries to give recognition to the Independence of Mizoram.

LALDENGA

Lalnunmawia	Lianzuala	Sainghaka
Thangkima	Lalhmingthanga	Zamawia
Bualhranga	Sakhawliana	Lalchhawna
Saikunga	Ngunhulha	Lallianzuala
Thangmawia	Vanmawia	Ngurchhina
Tlangchhuaka	Chuailokunga	V.L. Nghaka
Thangzika	Kawlremthanga	Hlunsanga
Vala	Thanghuta	Dokhuma
Thangkhuma	Hnuna	Thangbuaia
Thanghuaia	Lalluta	Lalchuanga
Thatthiauva	Vanhnuaithanga	Lalchhawna
Kapthanga	Challiana	Pachhunga

Rochhinga I	Rochhinga II	Vankunga
Vanlalliana	Thanglawra	Rangkhuma
Duma	Zanenga	Lalnundawta
Lalkhawliana	Ngurkunga	Lalhmuaka
Malsawma	Hrangchhinga	Zoramthanga
Chhunzawna	Rosanga	Lamputa
Vansiama	Vanlalzika	Zamanthanga
Rohmingthanga	Lalhruaia	Lalkhawhena

Appendix VI

THE ACCORD BETWEEN SUAKPUILAL AND THE BRITISH GOVERNMENT IN 1871

The Order of the Illustrious Government

Be it known to the Looshai Lall (Sookpuilal) and to all other Lalls, Muntrees and people of Looshai villages between the Tapai and Tiperrah Hills.

The Illustrious Government had laid down the following line of division:

From Chutturchurra to the mouth of Bhyrubeecherra, from the mouth of Bhyrucherra to Shyrubee Tillah from Bhyrubee Tillah to Kolosep Tillah to Noonvai Hills from Noonvai Hills to Kobocherra Mookh which falls to Sonai Nuddee, and it has ordered that the country to the north of the said line shall be called Cachar and the Marthinlong or Northern Looshai Lands; on the other side of that line of division shall be called the Looshai Hills. The name Marthinlong or Northern Looshai include those people who drink the water of the Taovai, Tipai, Tuirel or Sonai, Tinpar or Rukni, Sinlong, or Dullessur and Kloong Doong or Guttur.

The Illustrious Government has further ordered that (Sookpuilal) and all other Looshai Lalls, Muntrees, and people shall not in anyway injure or annoy any of the people of Sylhet or Cachar.

If any Looshai suffers any injury or annoyance at the hands of Cachar or Syhlet people, and wishes to have his wrongs redressed, he must take a request to that effect to the Burra Sahib (Deputy Commissioner) of Cachar, who has been ordered by Government to do justice in such cases.

The Lalls and Muntrees of the Looshais shall be answerable for the safety of all merchants and wood-cutters who go to the Looshai Hills to trade or cut timbers.

There are, as is known, various hill tribes known as Simthinglong drinking water of the river flowing to the South. If they or the people dwelling in the east of the Tipai are about to attack or annoy any people of Cachar or Sylhet, and if Sookpuilal, etc., know of it and cannot prevent them from passing through their villages, then Sookpuilal, etc., must at once given information to the Burra Sahib (Deputy Commissioner) of Cachar.

If a dispute arises between Sookpuilal, etc., and the people of the Rajahs or Manipur or Tiperrah, he or they may inform the Burra Sahib (Deputy Commissioner) of Cachar, who will endeavour to get the matter enquired into.

When the Burra Sahib of Cachar or any Government Officer who may be deputed by him goes to visit the Looshai Hills, Sookpuilal should meet him in person or by Deputy at some place to be appointed from time to time within the hills.

If in any year no European Government officer goes to the hills, then Sookpuilal, etc., shall send to the Burra Sahib (Deputy Commissioner) at Doodpate (Silchar) some respectable Looshais.

If at any time all the above orders of Government be not carried out, the said Government may revoke this *sunnud* and pass such orders as it thinks proper. But as long as Sookpuilal, etc., shall obey all these orders and any similar ones which the Government may issue from time to time for the preservation of peace on both sides of the above mentioned line, the Government will not interfere with the affairs of their villages, and will leave them in the undisturbed possession of their village land.

Dated the 16th January 1871

Note: The Government of India accorded their assent to the *sunnud vide* their letter No. 1544p, dated 22nd July, 1871.

Appendix VII

FIRST JULY 1976 PEACE ACCORD

1. A delegation of the underground Mizo National Front party led by Shri Laldenga and comprising of Sarvashri Tlangchhuaka, Chawngzuala, Biakchhunga, Biakvela, Zoramthanga and Rualchhina had a series of discussion with Shri S.L. Khurana. Home Secretary, Shri S.K. Chhiber, Lieut. Governor of Mizoram and Shri M.L. Kampani, Joint Secretary (North-East) representing the Government of India.
2. The MNF delegation acknowledged that Mizoram is an integral part of India and conveyed to the Government of India their resolve to accept a settlement of all problems in Mizoram within the framework of the Constitution of India.
3. In order to bring about a climate of understanding and an atmosphere of peace and tranquillity in Mizoram at the earliest, the delegation agreed to abjure violence and suspend all activities. In furtherance of the above objectives, the underground delegation agreed to collect all underground personnel with their arms and ammunition inside mutually agreed camps within

one month after their establishment and also agreed to hand over arms and ammunition to the Government of India.

4. The Government of India also decided to suspend operations, thereafter, by the security forces. Such suspension, however, would not apply to operations against underground personnel attempting to cross international border and the maintenance of law and order.
5. It was agreed to continue the talks further.

(Laldenga)
July 1, 1976

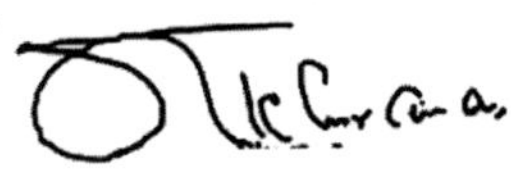

(S.L. Khurana)
July 1, 1976

Note: After ten odd years of insurgency Mizoram enters into an era of peace and progress. Reproduced above is text of the agreement signed by Shri Laldenga, on behalf of the MNF and Shri S.L. Khurana, Home Secretary representing the Government of India. The dark chapter of hardship and suffering is now over. Let us get on with the task of NATION BUILDING with zeal and dedication.

Appendix VIII

(Confidential)

AGREEMENT BETWEEN THE INDIAN NATIONAL CONGRESS (I) AND THE MIZO NATIONAL FRONT, MIZORAM

The Government of India under the leadership of the Prime Minister Shri Rajiv Gandhi has brought about a situation wherein the long years of disturbed conditions in Mizoram are being brought to an end. The Memorandum of Settlement is being signed between the Government of India and Shri Laldenga, President of the Mizo National Front to give shape to this effort to assure peace and prosperity in Mizoram within the framework of the Constitution of India. Shri Laldenga has pledged to bring the MNF into the mainstream of the Indian polity and irrevocably commit it to strive for a strong and united India.

In order to further strengthen to resolve and to enable a smooth and orderly transition, the Indian National Congress (I) and the MNF headed by Shri Laldenga agree to form a coalition Government. This decision shall be implemented in the following manner soon after the members of the MNF who are underground lay down their arms and join the national mainstream.

1. On a date agreed to between Shri Laldenga and the

Government of India, Shri Lal Thanhawla, the present Congress (I) Chief Minister will submit his resignation and Shri Laldenga will be elected the leader of the Government of Mizoram and be sworn in as the Chief Minister there.

2. Shri Lal Thanhawla, the present Chief Minister will be sworn as the Deputy Chief Minister.
3. In addition to the Deputy Chief Minister, four members of the Congress (I) party shall be made Ministers of the new Government.
4. In addition to the Chief Minister, three members from the MNF party will be made Ministers.
5. The name of the Ministers will be nominated by the respective political parties and the Chief Minister will propose them to the Lt. Governor.
6. All issues concerning the formation and induction of this new Government will be decided mutually by the Chief Minister and the Deputy Chief Minister.
7. In order to smoothen the function of the coalition Government, a Coordination Committee will be constituted consisting of the following :

(a) Shri Lal Denga — Chairman
(b) Shri Lal Thanhawla — Vice Chairman
(c) Two members of the Congress Party
(d) Two members of the MNF Party

This committee will take into consideration all matters concerning the party and the Government which either of the political parties may deem necessary to bring for its consideration in order to help smooth functioning of the Government and to bring better coordination between the Congress (I) and the MNF.

8. This Coalition Government will continue to function till such date when the President is satisfied that normalcy has returned and the holding of election has become feasible.
9. In the event of any difference arising between the two parties in the functioning of the Government or relationship between the parties they would seek the help of the Hon'ble Prime Minister to resolve the same.

[Laldenga]	[Arjun Singh]
President	Vice President
Mizo National Front	Indian National Congress

25th June, 1986

Appendix IX

MEMORANDUM OF SETTLEMENT

Preamble

1. Government of India have all along been making earnest efforts to bring about an end to the disturbed conditions in Mizoram and to restore peace and harmony.
2. Towards this end, initiative was taken by the late Prime Minister, Smt. Indira Gandhi. On the acceptance by Shri Laldenga on behalf of the Mizo Nationalist Front (MNF) of the two conditions, namely, cessation of violence by MNF and holding of talks within the framework of the Constitution of India, a series of discussion were held with Shri Laldenga. Settlement on various issues reached during the course of the talks is incorporated in the following paragraphs.

Restoration of Normalcy

3.1. With a view to restoring peace and normalcy in Mizoram, the MNF party, on their part, undertakes within the agreed time-frame, to take all necessary steps to end all underground activities, to bring about all underground personnel of the MNF with their arms, ammunition and equipment to ensure their return to civil life, to abjure violence and generally to help in the process of restoration of normalcy. The modalities of bringing out all underground personnel and the deposit of arms, ammunition and equipment will be as worked out. The implementation of the foregoing will be under the supervision of the Central Government.

3.2. The MNF party will take immediate steps to amend its Articles of Association so as to make them conform to the provision of law.

3.3. The Central Government will take steps for the resettlement and rehabilitation of underground MNF personnel coming overground after considering the steps proposed in this regard by the Government of Mizoram.

3.4. The MNF undertakes not to extend any support to Tripura/Tribal National Volunteers (TNV), People's Liberation Army of Manipur (PLA) and any other such groups, by way of training, supply of arms or providing protection or in any other manner.

Legal, Administrative and Other Steps

4.1. With a view to satisfying the desires and aspirations of all sections of the people of Mizoram, the Government will initiate measures to confer Statehood on the Union Territory of Mizoram, subject to the other stipulations contained in this Memorandum of Settlement.

4.2. To give effect to the above, the necessary legislative and administrative measures will be undertaken, including those for the amendment of the Constitution and other laws for the conferment of Statehood as aforesaid to come into effect on a date to be notified by the Central Government.

4.3. The Amendments aforesaid shall provide, among other things, for the following:

(i) The territory of Mizoram shall consist of the territory specified in Section 6 of the North Eastern Areas (Reorganisation) Act 1971.

(ii) Notwithstanding anything contained in the Constitution, no Act of Parliament in respect of :

(a) Religious or social practices of the Mizos,

(b) Mizo Customary law or procedure,

(c) Administration of Civil and Criminal Justice involving decisions according to Mizo Customary Law.

shall apply to the State of Mizoram unless the Legislative Assembly of Mizoram by a resolution so decides:

Provided that nothing in this clause shall apply to any Central Act in force in Mizoram immediately before the appointed day.

(iii) Article 170, Clause (1) shall, in relation to the Legislative Assembly of Mizoram, have effect as if for the word 'sixty', the word 'forty' has been substituted.

5. Soon after the Bill for conferment of Statehood becomes law, and when the President is satisfied

that normalcy has returned and that conditions conducive to the holding of free and fair elections exist, the process of holding elections to the Legislative Assembly will be initiated.

6. (a) The Centre will transfer resources to the new Government keeping in view the change in status from a Union Territory to a State and this will include resources to cover the revenue gap for the year.

   (b) Central assistance for Plan will be fixed taking note of any residuary gap in resources so as to sustain the approved Plan outlay and the pattern of assistance will be as in the case of special category States.

7. Border trade in locally produced or grown agricultural commodities could be allowed under a scheme to be formulated by the Central Government, subject to international arrangement with neighbouring countries.

8. The Inner Line Regulations, as now in force in Mizoram, will not be amended or repealed without consulting the State Government.

Other Matters

9. The rights and privileges of the minorities in Mizoram as envisaged in the Constitution, shall continue to be preserved and protected and their social and economic advancement shall be ensured.

10. Steps will be taken by the Government of Mizoram at the earliest to review and codify the existing

customs, practices, laws or other usages relating to the matters specified in clauses (a) to (d) of para 4.3 (I) of the Memorandum, keeping in view that an individual Mizo may prefer to be governed by Acts of Parliament dealing with such matters and which are of general application.

11. The question of the unification of Mizo inhabited areas of other States to form one administrative unit was raised by the MNF delegation. It was pointed out to them, on behalf of the Government of India, that Article 3 of the Constitution of India prescribes the procedure in this regard but that the Government cannot make commitment in this respect.

12. It was also pointed out on behalf of the Government that as soon as Mizoram becomes a State,
    (i) the provisions of Part XVII of the Constitution will apply and the State will be at liberty to adopt any one or more of the language in use in the State as the language to be used for all or any of the official purposes of the State;
    (ii) it is open to the State to move for the establishment of a separate University in the State in accordance with the prescribed procedure;
    (iii) in the light of the Prime Minister's statement at the joint conference of the Chief Justices, Chief Ministers and Law Ministers held at New Delhi on 31st August, 1985, Mizoram will be entitled to have a High Court of its own, if it so wishes.

13. (a) It was noted that there is already a scheme in force for payment of *ex gratia* amount to heirs/dependents of persons who were killed during

disturbances in 1966, and thereafter in the Union Territory of Mizoram. Arrangement will be made to expeditiously disburse payment to those eligible persons who had already applied but who had not been made such payments so far.

(b) It was noted that consequent on verification done by a joint team of officers, the Government of India had already made arrangements for payment of compensation in respect of damage to crops; buildings destroyed/damaged during the action in Mizoram and rental charges of buildings and lands occupied by the Security Forces. There may, however, be some claims which were preferred and verified by the above team but have not yet been settled. These pending claims will be settled expeditiously. Arrangement will also be made for payment of pending claims of rental charges for land/ buildings occupied by the Security Forces.

Sd/-
(LALDENGA)
On behalf of
Mizo National Front

Sd/-
(R.D. PRADHAN)
Home Secretary
Government of India

Sd/-
(LALKHAMA)
Chief Secretary
Government of Mizoram

Date : 30th June, 1986
Place : New Delhi

Profiles

Pu Lal Thanhawla

Who sacrificed his Chief Ministership for the cause of Peace

1.	Name	: Lal Thanhawla
2.	Date of birth	: 19th May, 1942
3.	Place of birth	: Presbyterian Hospital Durtlang, Aizawl, Mizoram, India.
4.	Present Address	: Chief Minister's Bungalow, McDonald Hill, Zarkawt, Aizawl, Mizoram, India.
5.	Permanent Address	: A/14, Zarkawt Main Street, Aizawl, Mizoram, India.
6.	Educational Qualification	: Bachelor of Arts.
7.	Marital status	: Married.

(a) Name of spouse : Lal Riliani.

(b) Number of children : One son and three daughters.

8. Political Party Affiliation : Indian National Congress.

9. Hobby : Reading and Gardening.

10. Special interest

(a) *Games & Sports* : A keen sportsman represented High School, College, Mizoram and Assam in Football and Hockey. Play Badminton, Carrom, Volley Ball, etc. Was founder-President, Mizoram Sports Association; Mizoram Football Association; Founder-President, Mizoram Hockey Association. Founder-Secretary, Mizoram Boxing Association. Started Mizoram Olympic Association in Mizoram and President till date. Chairman, North East Olympic Commission (under Indian Olympic Association). Member, Executive Council, Indian Olympic Association. Founder-Secretary, Aizawl Amateur Athletic Club.

(b) *Journalism* : Was Founder-President, Mizoram Journalists Association. Was correspondent, *The Assam Tribune*. Was Founder-Editor, Mizo *Aw-Mizo vernacular daily*. Was Editor of Congress Party daily *Remna Palai*.

11. Social Activities/Experience

(a) Started Young Mizo Association in Zarkawt Veng, Life Member, Central Young Mizo Association.

(b) Was Secretary, Central Information Forum.

(c) Was Founder-Secretary, Aizawl Dramatic and Cultural Society.

(d) Was Chairman, Literacy Committee, National Development Council, India.

(e) Was Vice President, Prohibition Council of India, New Delhi.

(f) Member, Congress Working Committee; and President, Mizoram Pradesh Congress Committee since 1973 till date.

(g) Was Member, Ninth Finance Commission of India.

(h) Member, The Shillong Club Ltd. and Country Club of India, Hyderabad, New Delhi.

(i) Life Member, Evangelical Fellowship of India and Bible Society of India

12. Favourite Pastime and Recreation:

 (a) Listening to soft music, blues, folk songs, oldies and classical music. Reading books and magazines on various topics.

 (b) Visit to Gym and Health Club.

13. *Countries Visited* : Europe, United States of America (including Hawaii), United Arab Emirates and its neighbouring Arab countries, China, Thailand, Singapore, Japan, Malaysia, Hongkong, etc.

14. Political Activities:

 (a) Joined the Indian National Congress in December 1967. Appointed Secretary, Mizo District Congress Committee.

 (b) Appointed General Secretary when Mizo District attained Union Territory and District

Congress Committee was upgraded to Pradesh Congress Committee.

(c) Was first elected President, Mizoram Pradesh Congress Committee in 1973 and held the post till date, except for brief period.

(d) Mizoram was afflicted with insurgency for 20 years. He initiated peace talk between the underground Mizo National Front and the Government of India. Voluntarily offered his Chief Ministership to the underground leader to usher in lasting peace and tranquillity in Mizoram. Accordingly, Mizoram Accord was signed between the Underground Mizo National Front and the Government of India under the leadership of Shri Rajiv Gandhi, Prime Minister.

15. Dates of election and period :

(a) First elected to the State Assemby in 1978 and became Opposition Group Leader.

(b) Re-elected in 1979 after Mizoram was under brief spell of President's Rule and became Leader of Opposition Group again.

(c) Elected in 1984 and became Chief Minister. Resigned voluntarily in August 1986 to pave the way for signing of Mizoram Accord for ushering in lasting peace in Mizoram, but was compelled by Rajiv Gandhi to become Dy. Chief Minister.

(d) Elected again in 1987 and became Leader of Opposition. Government led by Laldenga, MNF dissolved after being reduced to minority and imposed President's Rule.

(e) Elected again in 1989 and became Chief Minister.

(f) Re-elected in 1993 and became Chief Minister.

(g) Elected again in 2003 and became Leader of the Opposition.

(h) Elected again in 2008 and became the Chief Minister for the fourth time.

16. Sports :

(a) He has led Indian delegation of Indian Sports Administrators to Kuwait City in "International Conference on Sports and the Environment".

(b) He has also led Indian Wushu Team to Rome at International Wushu Competition and bagged 4 Gold, 5 Silver and Bronze medals.

(c) He has also represented the Indian Olympic Association in Singapore on "International Conference on Sports and Cultural Relations".

(d) He has represented the Indian Olympic Association in the Olympic in 2004 at Athens.

17. Awards :

He has been recipient of a number of Awards including "National Citizens Award" in 1994 from Mother Teresa; and "Mother Teresa Lifetime Achievement Award" in 2009. Association; Founder- President, Mizoram Hockey Association. Founder-Secretary, Mizoram Boxing Association. Started Mizoram Olympic Association in Mizoram and President till date.

Pu Laldenga

Founder President of Mizo National Front

Born on June 11, 1927 at Pukpui Village near Lunglei. After M.E. School at Serkawn, he went to join Assam Training School, Jowai. Joined the Army in 1944 and became Havildar Clerk. In 1953, he joined Mizo District Council as Accountant-cum-Cashier. In 1958, he founded the Mizo Cultural Society which was greatly valued by the public. In the beginning of 1960, leaving his District Council job, he formed Mizo National Famine Front to combat with the raging famine which was overtaking Mizoram then. The organisation became political body on October 22, 1961 by dropping the word 'Famine' and the MNF was thus born, with Laldenga as Founder President.

On March 1, 1966, MNF declared Mizoram as independent country and as a result MNF began its activities and operation in an underground manner. After 20 years of underground movement, Peace Accord was signed by the MNF and the Government of India on 30th June, 1986. In the Interim Government, Laldenga became

Chief Minister on September 21, 1986. In the 1987 Elections, he won from both Sateek and Aizawl North-II Constituencies. In February 1987, he became the first Chief Minister of Mizoram State. He died of cancer on July 7, 1990 at London Heathrow Airport while on his way home from New York. Full State funeral was accorded to him by Government of Mizoram on 13th July, 1990.

Source: Emergence of Mizoram 2010 (P. Lalnithanga, IAS Retired)

Students Procession on Zoram Ni, 5th March, 2012, in protest against the Indian Air Force Jet Fighter bombing Aizawl and other places. At Aizawl 13 people were killed. Zoram Ni has been observed as Thanks Giving Day to God and Mizo Unity Day

Index